GREAT HIKES

IN THE

POCONOS

AND

NORTHEAST

PENNSYLVANIA

GREAT HIKES

IN THE

POCONOS

AND

NORTHEAST

PENNSYLVANIA

Boyd and Linda Newman

STACKPOLE
BOOKS

Published by
STACKPOLE BOOKS
5067 Ritter Road
Mechanicsburg, PA 17055
www.stackpolebooks.com

Printed in the United States of America

Cover design by Caroline Stover
Cover photo by John Serrao
Illustrations by Erin O'Toole

10 9 8 7 6 5 4 3 2 1

First edition

Library of Congress Cataloging-in-Publication Data

Newman, Boyd, 1941–
Great hikes in the Poconos and northeast Pennsylvania / Boyd and Linda Newman.
p. cm.
Includes index.
ISBN 0-8117-2773-4 (alk. paper)
1. Hiking—Pennsylvania—Guidebooks. 2. Trails—Pennsylvania—Guidebooks. I. Newman, Linda A., 1943– II. Title.

GV199.42.P4 N49 2000
917.48'20444—dc21

99-049064

To Margaret Hughes, Linda's mom, a really fine and classy person. She took care of two trail-weary hikers with home-cooked dinners, hot showers, and a soft bed. She was a great researcher. Most of all, she provided and continues to provide love and support—for the book and in our lives.

CONTENTS

APPENDIXES

INTRODUCTION

Pennsylvania is a great hiking state. A recent federal study shows that the New England and Mid-Atlantic states have gained 23 million acres of forest in the last ninety years. And more of those acres are in Pennsylvania than in any other state. Pennsylvania has almost 17 million forested acres and over 3,000 miles of hiking trails.

Some of the best hiking in Pennsylvania is in the northeastern part of the state, where forests have been reclaimed from abandoned farming and logging operations. Many of these hikes are in relatively remote areas, where you are unlikely to encounter other hikers. The terrain is varied and rich in history. Several wildlife species, such as the coyote, bobcat, fox, and turkey, have staged recoveries. Almost 70 percent of the black bear population of Pennsylvania is in the isolated forests of the north-central and northeastern part of the state.

We organized the hikes into four regions, distinct in terrain, geology, history, and animal and plant life. How did we happen to pick these particular hikes from scores of other possibilities? First, each hike offers something special: an outstanding view, a unique geologic feature, a bit of history, or unusual plant or animal life. Next, whenever possible, we chose a circuit hike. It's a lot more interesting when you don't know exactly what's ahead, and your chance of seeing animals also improves dramatically. Third, we just love waterfalls. You don't have to be an authority on anything to enjoy the sight and sound of falling water. There are over fifty falls in these hikes. Streams, rapids, ponds, swamps, and lakes are also mesmerizing, so there are lots of them, too.

The hikes, with one exception (Tannersville Cranberry Bog, chosen for unique ecology), are all over 2 miles in length. Nineteen hikes are under 5 miles, twenty-one more are 5 to 10 miles, and there are two over 10 miles long. We also included a section of nature hikes, all less than 2 miles in length, as well as an appendix of fifteen trails that are accessible in whole or in part to wheelchair hikers.

POCONOS

Pocono history is written on the landscape. Retreating glaciers scoured the earth, leaving behind bogs, glacial "kettle" lakes, and, in some places, flora and fauna more typical of Canada. Abandoned foundations of farmhouses and stone row fences tell of earnest yet failed attempts to eke out a living from the rocky, poorly drained soil. Today, the region prospers again with the ski and tourist industries. Still, there are many fascinating wild places yet to explore.

RIDGE AND VALLEY PROVINCE

Blue, or Kittatinny, Mountain is the southernmost ridge of the Appalachian Mountains, which run in a generally northeast to southwest band across Pennsylvania. Two hundred eighty million years ago, geologic forces lifted and folded deep layers of sedimentary rocks. Erosion wore down and continues to shape these mountains into knife edges of hard sandstone and granite at the top of narrow ridges. These steep, rocky slopes largely escaped farming and industrial development and have remained wild and forested. Hawk Mountain is a good example of these geologic forces at work and is along the major flyway for migrating birds.

SUSQUEHANNA RIVER VALLEY

The Susquehanna River was an important trade route long before early settlers arrived. Native Americans were driven west; their stories are told at Frances Slocum and Salt Spring State Parks. Railroads supported industrial development—coal, timber, and tanning. Streams were dammed to supply ice to growing population centers in Wilkes-Barre and Scranton. The valleys of the Susquehanna also support a unique river and floodplain ecology.

NORTH WOODS

The North Woods, or Endless Mountains, of Pennsylvania's northern tier were once lumbered over. Former stands of white pine and hemlock have been replaced by oak, maple, and black cherry. Now some forests are threatened by insects, such as the elm spanworm and gypsy moth, and an overpopulation of deer that overbrowse young trees and the understory. Nevertheless, these woods are recovering. Most of these hikes involve some fairly strenuous climbing, more so than in the gently rolling Poconos.

HIKE DETAILS

At the beginning of each hike, we list information to help you decide which hike to do when. We hope you do them all.

- **Distance.** The length of each hike is given in miles.
- **Elevation.** Elevation refers to the cumulative gain in elevation for each hike; this may consist of one long uphill climb or several ups (and downs).
- **Time to hike.** This is just an average. If you walk faster or slower than average, adjust the time accordingly.
- **Surface.** This information is included to help you decide on footwear. Combining information on hike length, elevation change, and trail surface also allows you to judge difficulty.
- **Interesting features.** Each hike was included because of some unique or interesting characteristics.
- **Facilities.** Information is provided on the availability of water, rest rooms, and picnic facilities.
- **Hunting.** This tells you whether hunting is allowed on the trail.
- **Directions.** Directions to each trailhead are given from a community and major highway (including exit number, when applicable) near the community. The locator map on page 6 shows the referenced major highways and communities. Each hike is indicated on the map with a number that corresponds to its number in the text. Simply find the hike and your own approximate location on the map, and pick up the directions at the appropriate point.
- **Coordinates.** For high-tech hikers, we included the latitude and longitude at the start of each hike. If you (or your car) are equipped with Global Positioning System (GPS) technology, this information may help you locate the trailhead from the highway or trail.

ADVICE

Safety

• **Hunting.** For hikes in state game lands, national or state parks, or anywhere hunting is permitted, keep in mind hunting seasons. Large-game season generally runs from the Monday before Thanksgiving to the first week of January. Small-game season runs a few weeks before and after. (No hunting is allowed in Pennsylvania on Sundays.) Don't hike in hunting areas during game seasons, especially large game. If you happen to hear gunshots while hiking, don't be shy. Call out loudly or blow a whistle to signal your presence.

• **Essentials.** Always take water, even on a short hike. Do not drink from streams, no matter how clean they appear. For a longer hike, include a snack or lunch. Take a map and a compass, and know how to read both.

• **Lyme disease.** Ticks can carry Lyme disease. Carefully inspect skin and clothing when you return to your car, and contact a doctor if you develop a rash or unexplained fatigue after a hike. A vaccine for Lyme disease is available and is recommended for those who spend much time outdoors in tick-infested areas.

• **Animals.** Avoid strange-acting or friendly wild animals. They may be infected with rabies. You may see a black bear; if you do, enjoy the experience from a distance. If a bear appears threatening, back away slowly. Remember, a bear can outrun you. In rocky areas, watch for snakes, especially if you are using your hands for climbing.

• **Weather.** During a thunderstorm with lightning, seek shelter at a low elevation and avoid tall trees.

• **Company.** Hike alone only for short distances in well-traveled areas. We recommend taking along a hiking companion. Always let someone know where you are going.

Clothing, Boots, Equipment

We recommend lightweight cotton pants and a long-sleeved shirt for protection against poison ivy, stinging and biting insects, scratches, and briers. If you accidentally kick up a hornets' nest, as we have done, long sleeves and pants may protect you from serious injury. In cool weather, dress in layers. Take along dry socks and boots for those hikes requiring stream crossings, especially in cool weather. For most of these hikes, especially those described as rocky or with significant elevation change, wear sturdy, well-fitting boots with ankle protection. Use insect repellent, sunscreen, and a hat, depending on the season.

This equipment is sufficient for the day hikes in this book. For an overnight hike, consult other references for a more complete list.

As Henry David Thoreau said, "Methinks that the moment my legs begin to move, my thoughts begin to flow." May your legs move and your thoughts flow in Penn's Woods.

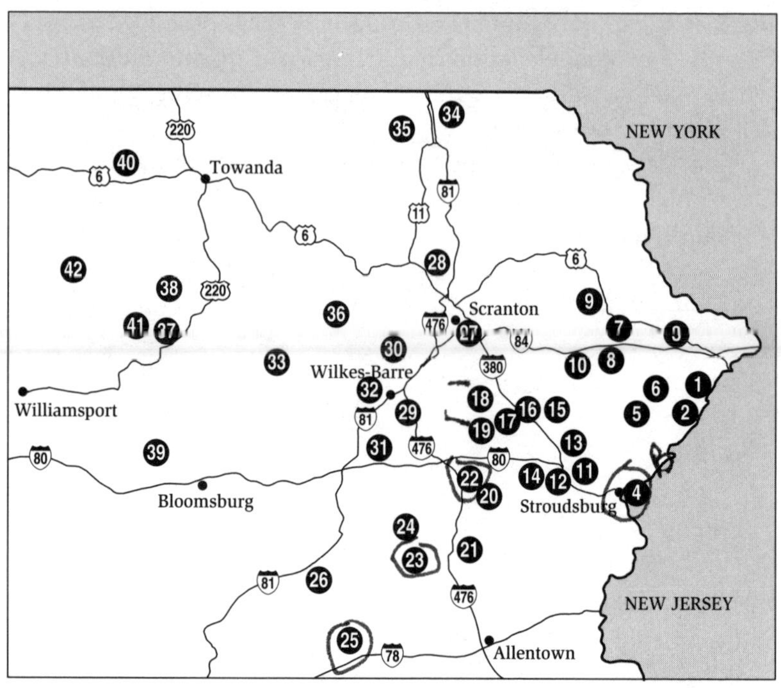

1. Dingmans Falls
2. Pocono Environmental Education Center
3. Shohola Falls
4. Delaware Water Gap
5. Pennel Run
6. Stillwater Natural Area
7. Blooming Grove 4-H Trail
8. Bruce Lake Natural Area
9. Shuman Point Natural Area
10. Promised Land State Park
11. Tannersville Cranberry Bog
12. Big Pocono State Park
13. Devils Hole
14. Wolf Swamp and Deep Lake
15. Tobyhanna State Park
16. Gouldsboro State Park
17. Brady's Lake
18. Big Pine Hill
19. Choke Creek Trail
20. Margy's Trail
21. Beltzville State Park
22. Hickory Run State Park
23. Switchback Railroad
24. Glen Onoko Run
25. Hawk Mountain
26. Locust Lake State Park
27. Lake Scranton
28. Lackawanna State Park
29. Seven Tubs Nature Area
30. Frances Slocum State Park
31. Nescopeck Ponds Loop
32. Riverside Commons
33. Ricketts Glen State Park
34. Great Bend
35. Salt Springs State Park
36. Joe Gmiter Trail
37. Eagles Mere
38. Worlds End State Park
39. Chilisuagi Trail
40. Mt. Pisgah
41. Loyalsock Trail
42. Cherry Ridge Trail

PART ONE

POCONOS

Wayne, Pike, and Monroe Counties

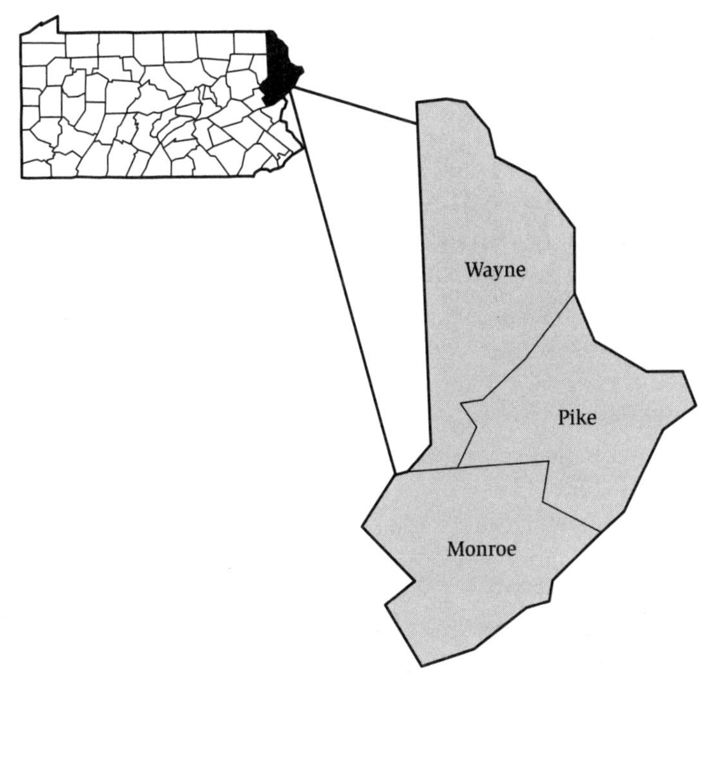

1. DINGMANS FALLS

Distance	5.2 miles
Elevation	380 feet
Time to hike	3 hours
Surface	Rocky, unblazed trail; wooden boardwalk, steps, and viewing platforms
Interesting features	Five waterfalls; the highest, 130-foot Dingmans Falls, is the highest in Pennsylvania
Facilities	Water, rest rooms, picnic facilities at Childs Recreation Site; water, rest rooms at Dingmans; no camping or swimming
Hunting	No

Directions

From I-84 (Exit 9) near the New Jersey–New York line:

1. South on PA 739 for 12.8 miles to Silver Lake Road
2. Turn right on Silver Lake Road for 1.5 miles
3. Turn left at parking lot

Coordinates 41°14'15"N; 74°54'53"W

This hike is a delight to the waterfall lover. At Childs Recreation Site, part of the Delaware Water Gap National Recreation Area, you hike through a deep hemlock gorge and circle three beautiful waterfalls. From there, hike along Dingmans Creek to Dingmans Falls, nearby Silverthread Falls, and the Visitors Center.

From the parking lot, walk past the picnic tables toward Dingmans Creek and Fulmer Falls. Sheer rock walls at the base of the falls provide the perfect misty environment for ferns, mosses, and liverworts. Turn right at a viewing platform on wooden steps to follow the creek upstream to Factory Falls. Ruins of an old mill are on your right. The mill was built in 1825 by Joseph Brooks from Yorkshire, England. His plan was to raise sheep and process the wool at the mill, with the power supplied by Factory Falls. Unfortunately, the sheep were easy prey for wolves or were poisoned by eating sheep laurel, and the mill was abandoned.

Continue to walk upstream, passing a wooden bridge over the creek. At the next bridge, cross the stream. Turn left downstream to view Factory and Fulmer Falls from the south side. Steep wooden

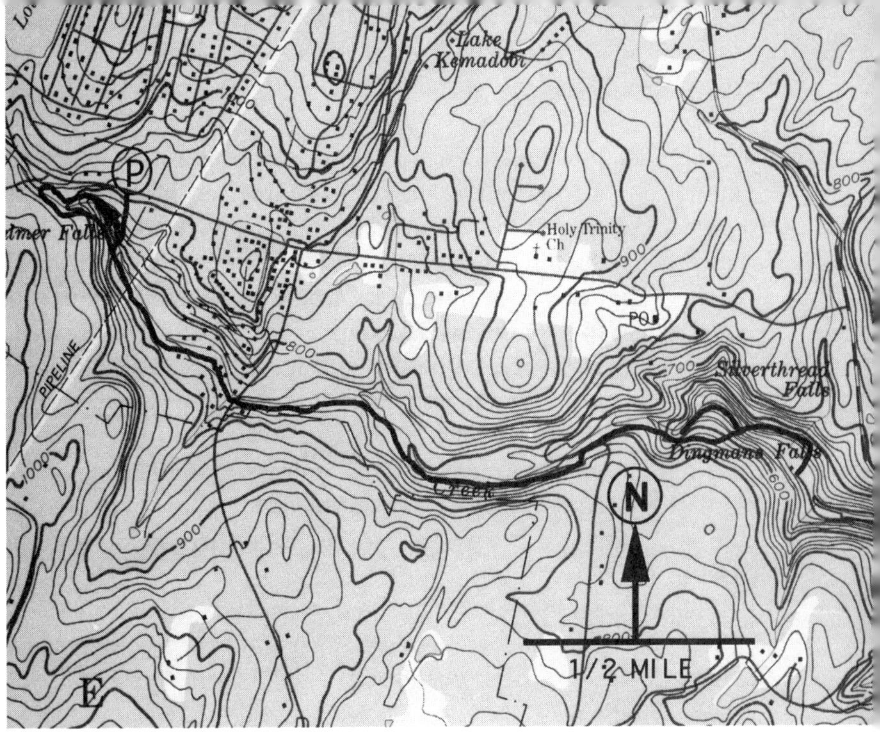

steps and platforms provide excellent views of the creek and falls. A bridge crosses the creek directly over Deer Leap Falls. Continue ahead to the next bridge, but do not cross it. Walk past the wooden fence, leave the boardwalk, and continue to walk downstream, staying on the south side.

The trail to Dingmans Falls is not blazed and clings to the hillside. The first section is the most demanding part of the hike. Take the easiest route downstream on interlacing paths. Cross a grassy pipeline cut, then several small tributaries on stepping-stones. You cross a small stream on a log or rusty culvert just before crossing Milford Road (State Route 2001) at 1.5 miles. Follow an abandoned woods road a short distance. When it turns to the right, turn left on the trail toward the stream. The hemlocks and rhododendrons provide cool shade. Occasional stands of young beech allow enough light for ferns. You reach a bridge closed to traffic on Doodle Hollow Road. Stay on the south side, as private property lies on the opposite stream bank.

Soon you hear and see Dingmans Falls. On our last visit, the Upper Falls Trail was closed for construction, with a sign stating, "Area closed to public use." If this area is still closed on your visit, turn right (southwest) up an old woods road beside a steep ravine. Continue on the road for 1,000 feet until a T intersection with another woods road. Turn left, cross a small tributary, then turn left again on a faint trail along the stream. Bushwhack northeast a short distance across a hemlock slope. You can look down a precipitous drop of about 150 feet to the boardwalk and gravel service road to the right. Bear right along the ridge line away from the falls and angle down the slope southwest for an easier descent to the road. Turn left on the service road—a short distance to the boardwalk.

If the Upper Falls Trail is open on your visit, continue to a viewing platform. Then walk down steep steps to the base of Dingmans Falls and follow the boardwalk trail to Silverthread Falls and the Visitors Center.

The trails were heavily damaged by winter storms in 1997–98 but have been rebuilt even better than before. New wooden boardwalks and platforms lead past benches to 80-foot Silverthread and 130-foot Dingmans Falls. The Visitors Center is scheduled to reopen in late 1999.

Heavy rains and meltwater in spring generate the most dramatic flow of water over the falls. Dense rhododendrons create a tunnel on the trail and bloom in late June and July. On the coldest winter days, the waterfalls partially freeze and are particularly dramatic. However, Childs Park and Dingmans Falls should be visited separately in the winter because of treacherous slippery conditions on the unmaintained trail between the two parks.

Visit both falls, then retrace your steps to Childs Recreation Site, cross the bridge over Deer Leap Falls, and return to your car at 5.2 miles.

2. POCONO ENVIRONMENTAL EDUCATION CENTER

Distance	9.5 miles
Elevation	490 feet
Time to hike	4½ hours
Surface	Woods trail—shale, pine needles, rocky in places
Interesting features	60-foot-high waterfall, deep hemlock ravines, windswept ridges with mountain views, fossil pit
Facilities	Water, rest rooms, picnicking at the Visitors Center (get a map and sign in before beginning to hike)
Hunting	Yes

Directions

From I-84 (Exit 9) near the New Jersey–New York line:

1. South on PA 739 toward Dingmans Ferry for 13 miles to PA 209
2. Turn right (south) on PA 209 for 4.8 miles to Briscoe Mountain Road
3. Turn right on Briscoe Mountain Road for .8 mile to Emery Road
4. Bear right on Emery Road for .1 mile to Visitors Center

Coordinates 41°10'18"N; 74°54'52"W

The Pocono Environmental Education Center trails offer a wide variety of Pocono habitats: dry, windswept ridge; red pine plantation; farm fields reverting to woods; and swamps, ponds, and streams. Rock hounds will find shale and siltstone outcroppings containing fossils from millions of years ago at many locations along the trail.

Begin hiking on the yellow-blazed Sunrise Trail (running with the red-blazed Scenic Gorge Trail), to the left of the Visitors Center. Cross a small wooden bridge, heading north. At .2 mile, you pass a small building, a water pumping station, with a sign indicating "Confidence Courses" to the left. Continue ahead past blueberries, hemlocks, and small beech trees. At .5 mile, you reach a trail intersection; bear left, staying with the yellow blazes and leaving the red-blazed Scenic Gorge Trail. There are several intersecting trails

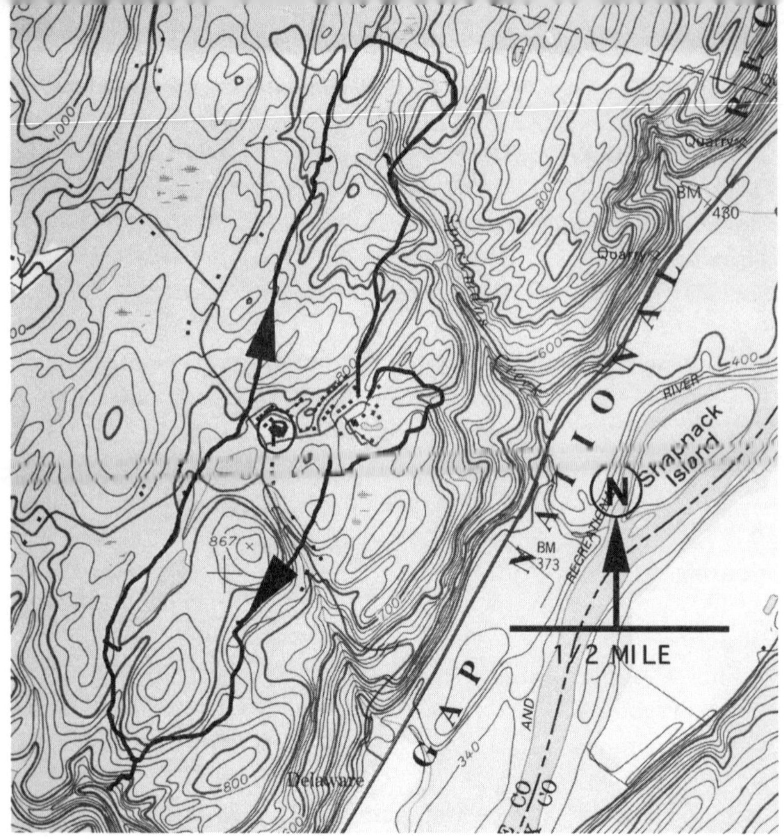

here, and the yellow blazes are faint. Watch closely for double yellow blazes, indicating turns.

At 1 mile, you briefly rejoin the red-blazed Sunrise Gorge Trail. Cross a stream and follow the yellow blazes on the opposite side. The Sunrise Gorge Trail turns right. Follow the yellow blazes left.

The trail here runs through a deep hemlock ravine, which ascends on a shale-covered trail through hardwoods and then sparser vegetation at higher elevations. Rock outcroppings alternate with descents to slow-moving streams and swamps. At 1.7 miles you are on a high rocky ledge, looking down 70 feet to a ravine. A rope has been conveniently tied to a tree root, which you can use to rappel down 20 feet. The rest of the way you can slide sitting down, or if you are surefooted, you may want to risk the slippery shale surface under your feet.

At 2.2 miles, pass the stone chimney and foundation remains of a farmhouse. A nearby farm pond is slowly filling with vegetation. Farming must have been difficult—Pocono potatoes (rocks) abound.

Step over another stream at a ravine and again climb out of the ravine to a ridge, then down again to a swampy area.

At 3 miles, cross a small stream and then a larger stream above a 15-foot-high waterfall and rejoin the red-blazed Sunrise Gorge Trail. Turn left, following the blazes along Alicia's Creek. The trail continues through a deep hemlock forest, then climbs out to second-growth hardwoods as you near the camping area.

You reach an asphalt road and a group of small cabins at 5 miles. Turn left at cabin 24. Pass two smaller cabins on the left side. Just before cabin 25, bear left through pine trees to find the blue-blazed Fossil Trail. Pass a small amphitheater with a campfire pit, along a small stream on the right. The trail heads steeply downhill to a shale rock outcropping on the left at 5.7 miles. A large trail sign indicates the types of fossils to be seen here. We found plenty of crinoids and fossilized plants imprinted with round circles (stems) and honeycombed with tiny holes (rootlets). You have to search harder to find the imprints of brachiopods and trilobites. Trilobites (such as *Phacops rana,* the official state fossil) are extinct jointed, legged animals related to crabs and insects. Do not remove any fossils from the site; leave them on the nearby logs for others to study.

Following the blazes, step over a small stream and head back uphill. At 6 miles, you reach a fairly confusing trail intersection. *Walk between two trees with blue blazes.*

On the left, pass a dense swamp. The standing water is dark from tannic acid from the surrounding hemlock trees and covered with a scum layer. When we were here five years earlier, it was an open pond. Vegetation is slowly invading the pond; notice the grassy plants rooted in water. Blue flag iris and other wetland flowers colonize the logs that have fallen in the pond. Pass a stone row fence and the foundation remains of another farmhouse on the left.

At 6.5 miles, reach an intersection with the orange-blazed Tumbling Waters Trail, and turn left. The trail ascends to Cedar Knoll, a rocky outcrop populated with red cedar, juniper, paper birch, scrub pine, and oak. You might find more fossils in the shale. Also notice deep scratches in the rocks; they are called glacial striations and were made by the rocks within the glacier as it moved over bedrock. At 6.7 miles, cross Briscoe Mountain Road, picking up the orange blazes on the other side. An old woods road leads to the remains of a cabin at Hermit's Hill at 7.4 miles. Here we spotted a bright scarlet tanager. Another .1 mile and you are rewarded with an excellent view of farmland to the southeast from the top of a narrow ridge, with steep drops on both sides.

Descending the ridge, at 8.2 miles you reach a side trail to two waterfalls on Mill Creek. The trail (.7 mile round-trip) leads by a series of steep switchbacks to a deep hemlock ravine with a lovely 60-foot waterfall plunging to a deep pool. There is another, smaller waterfall just downstream.

Rejoin the main trail, and at 9 miles you reach the top of the steep, aptly named Killer Hill. The white-blazed Two Pond Trail comes in from the right and joins the orange-blazed trail. From here on, the walking is easy on an old logging road, through even rows of a red pine plantation. The trees, planted about eighty years ago, grow tall and straight as they compete for sunlight. Red pine is not a native species and does not propagate well here. Little vegetation and few pine seedlings grow on the forest floor. At 9.2 miles, reach and pass a pretty lake, Pickerel Pond.

Shortly, cross another asphalt road, turning right for 100 feet to a bend in the road, where you spot the orange and white blazes on the other side. Cross Alicia's Creek, which drains Pickerel Pond, and follow it through thickets of honeysuckle and wild grapes. To your right are wetlands along a stone row fence with a lot of skunk cabbage.

Walk through a meadow reverting to woods. At 9.4 miles, you pass a fascinating "Ecology Cemetery" on the left. Samples of various materials with headstones indicate how long it takes each to decompose.

A groundhog at the edge of the meadow stopped to stare at us for a moment before hurrying into the high grass. Wildflowers fill the meadow all summer long.

Turn right on Two Ponds Trail on a boardwalk with a platform blind to view the wetlands you just passed. Warblers and catbirds frequent the thickets.

At 9.5 miles, return to the parking lot. The Visitors Center contains exhibits, rest rooms, water, a small library, and a nature-oriented gift shop.

3. SHOHOLA FALLS

Distance	8.2 miles
Elevation	360 feet
Time to hike	4 hours
Surface	Woods trail, game-lands road, grassy path
Interesting features	Shohola Falls and lake, observation tower, birding
Facilities	Water, rest rooms, picnic tables, grills near parking lot
Hunting	Yes

Directions

From I-84 (Exit 9) near the New Jersey–New York line:

1. North on PA 739 for .7 mile to Well Road
2. Turn right on Well Road (SR 1001) for 3.8 miles to US 6
3. Turn right (east) on US 6 for 2 miles to Shohola Falls Recreation Area parking lot, on the right side

Coordinates 41°23'30"N; 74°58'28"W

Shohola Lake covers 1,150 acres and is located within State Game Lands 180, which, at 11,372 acres, is one of the largest game lands in Pennsylvania. The terrain is rolling and wooded. Birders will find plenty of warblers in open areas adjoining the woods; waterfowl along the lake; and turkey, grouse, and pheasant at field edges.

Walk past the rest rooms, then turn left and follow the signs to the dam and overlooks. The trail leads through a picnic area and a meadow to the 25-foot dam. Follow the signs to turn left toward the falls just below the dam. The falls drop dramatically 100 feet over nine rocky, flat ledges and then cut through an 80-foot hemlock ravine through layers of shale and siltstone. A variety of mosses, ferns, and wildflowers have colonized the steep rock walls. The creek tumbles 200 feet in half a mile.

Continue to walk downstream on a rocky path, down wooden steps to a platform overlooking the falls and stream far below. Continuing on the woods path above the stream, you reach Old Route 6, which ends at a fence at the top of the gorge. Continue, crossing the creek on the bridge on US 6, and follow a trail on the opposite ridge

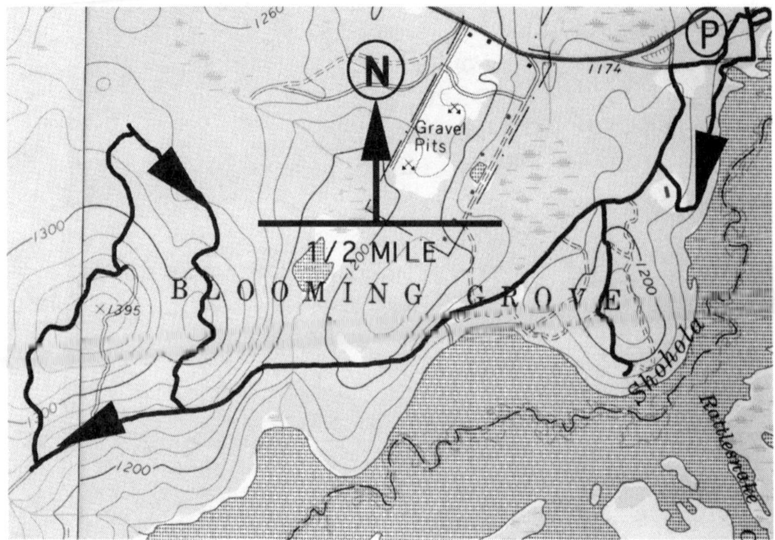

through a hemlock forest. Here you have an even better view of the falls head-on from another scenic overlook.

Walk back through the picnic area to the rest rooms and follow the sign reading, "To Boating," on a woods trail. Turn left at a T intersection toward the lake, staying on the mossy woods path. Cross a boat access road and continue on the woods trail. At a woods road turn left; there are marshy areas on both sides, which provide protected nesting sites for herons, ducks, and grebes. Turn right on a gravel two-track and walk past a maintenance building. Turn left on a game-lands road at 2 miles.

Continue on the road for .1 mile until you reach a pull-off on the left to an observation tower. A short grassy path leads to the 25-foot tower overlooking the lake. Just across the lake is a wildlife propagation area. Bald eagles and ospreys, nearly driven to extinction by high levels of DDT in the food chain, have been successfully reintroduced to the area at protected breeding sites here. The tower also offers a fine place for birders to view migrating waterfowl in the spring and fall.

Return to the road and turn left. At 2.7 miles, you reach a parking lot for a boat access ramp. Continue straight ahead past a metal gate on a gravel road, which is usually closed to traffic. The road parallels the lake for a short distance, then turns away from it, climbing

200 feet in a half mile. Wood-duck nesting boxes are placed at the edge of feedlots. There are dense clumps of shadbush (serviceberry) along the road that produce fragrant clusters of white flowers in May and purple fruit in July. We found a patch of wild lupines (purple flowers on stalks 12 inches high).

Just before a game-lands parking area on the left at 3.1 miles, you pass your return route, a grassy path on your right. Pass another trail on your right, then another culvert. Just before the top of a hill, at a rock culvert, turn right on the unsigned Horseshoe Trail, a grassy path (at 3.3 miles). The edge community of shadbush, wild grapes, and raspberries provides food and cover for birds. Turkeys feed on acorns in the woods but also like the insects and seeds found at the forest edge.

Favored by Ben Franklin as a good choice for our national bird, the turkey is found in every state but Alaska. Alas, the turkey is a victim of bad press. It is considered tasty but stupid, and calling someone a "dumb turkey" is hardly a compliment. Yet the eastern wild turkey has proved adaptable to the impact of humans on its environment. Its numbers are growing in Pennsylvania, while supposedly more intelligent animals such as elk, wolves, and mountain lions are extinct. And unlike other "snowbirds" (both feathered and not), the turkey is content to spend the whole year in Penn's Woods.

There are strawberries and apple trees, remnants of an old orchard, on the sunny path. Maples, chestnut oaks, small birch saplings, and ferns are in the woods just beyond the shrubs. At 3.7 miles, turn left (north) downhill on another grassy road just before the trail turns right, to the east. At 4.1 miles you reach an intersection with another grassy road. Make a sharp right (south). The trail is wet in places. At 4.9 miles, turn left on the gravel road, completing the loop begun at 3.3 miles. Follow your same route back to the parking lot at 8.2 miles.

4. DELAWARE WATER GAP

Distance	4.3 miles
Elevation	920 feet
Time to hike	2½ hours
Surface	Rocky trail, gravel road
Interesting features	Spectacular views of the Delaware Water Gap, the Appalachian Trail
Facilities	None
Hunting	Yes

Directions

From I-80 (Exit 53) near the New Jersey line:

1. South on PA 611 for .8 mile to Mountain Road
2. Turn right onto Mountain Road for .1 mile to Lake Road
3. Veer left on Lake Road, and park in the lot on the right side

Coordinates 40°58'55"N; 75°08'31"W

The Delaware River is the only major undammed, free-flowing river east of the Mississippi. It courses 35 miles through approximately 70,000 acres of recreational land in Pennsylvania and New Jersey. At its southern end, the river has cut through the Kittatinny Ridge, creating a narrow gorge—the Delaware Water Gap. On the Pennsylvania side, the ridge is called Mount Minsi; it faces Mount Tammany in New Jersey. This area was a popular resort site in the nineteenth century, with large hotels that catered to the upper class.

The hike to climb Mount Minsi begins at the south end of the parking lot. Look for the white blazes indicating the Appalachian Trail (AT); walk past a metal gate on a worn asphalt road through mixed hardwoods and conifers. To the left, just after the gate, you pass a small sinkhole, which remains wet and supports several large swamp white oaks. After another 200 feet you cross the dam on Caledonia Creek, which created Lake Lenape. Water lilies cover half the lake's surface. A .5-mile loop circles the lake, which is home to a variety of snakes, frogs, and turtles as well as waterbirds. Just after the lake, a trail splits off to the left and follows Caledonia Creek to a scenic overlook. Continue ahead on the white-blazed AT.

Walk uphill through an area thick with hemlocks and mountain laurel. In June and early July, the laurel is covered in pale pink

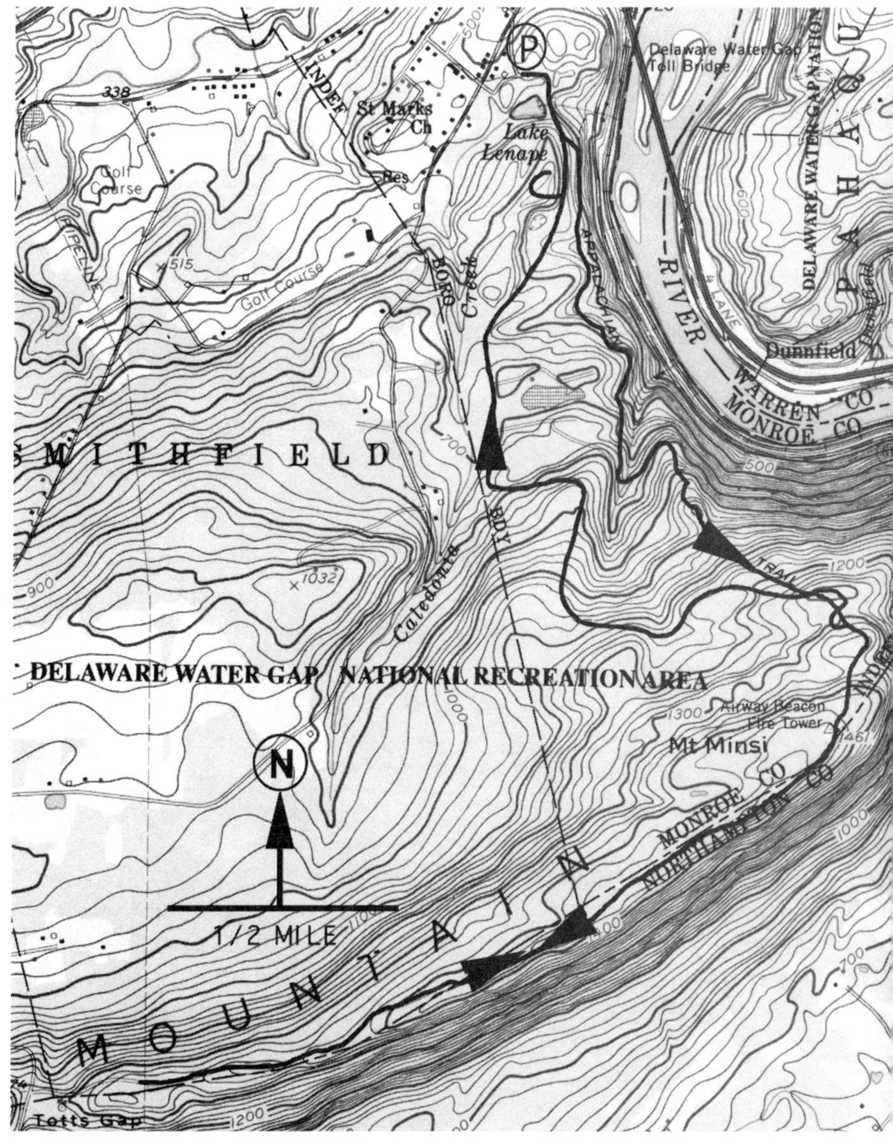

blooms. To the right, a rocky cliff steepens to about 100 feet; note what is supposed to have been an Indian shelter beneath a rocky ledge. At .2 mile, the white-blazed AT turns left, while the Mount Minsi Fire Road (your return route) continues straight ahead.

Turn left uphill on the AT through a thick forest of hemlock, laurel, and rhododendron. The trail becomes rockier. Impressive views of the Delaware River, I-80, and the bridge lie far below. Step over three small streams. At 1 mile, cross a larger stream on a log bridge.

You ascend on a trail that becomes ever steeper and rockier. Dense rhododendron crowd in and create a tunnel effect. Staying on the AT near the summit, cross the old Fire Road twice. The third time you encounter it, it joins the AT. As you follow the trail to turn left, the road peters out, but the AT continues to a rocky overlook in another two minutes (at 2 miles). The quartzite here has resisted erosion for 435 million years and caps weaker layers of shale underneath. Here the view of the Delaware Water Gap from an elevation of 1,360 feet is truly spectacular. Mount Tammany and New Jersey lie across the river. The river and the gap are over 1,000 feet below.

If you wish to extend your hike, continue on the AT. The trail continues uphill to the actual summit at 1,463 feet at the remains of an old fire tower and a small radio tower. The walking from here is a lot easier on a wide grassy road that follows the ridgeline. Short paths lead to the left for views of Pennsylvania farmland and mountains. Still on the AT, at Totts Gap you reach a gate and a microwave tower at 4.2 miles. A pipeline cut affords fine views to the north and south. The AT turns left and continues south to Georgia, or you can backtrack the way you came. This hike extension is not included in the total mileage given.

From the Delaware Water Gap overlook, backtrack the .1 mile down to where the AT splits off, but continue straight ahead on the Mount Minsi Fire Road for the walk back. This is easy walking, gently downhill. At 3 miles, a spring bubbles up from some rocks to your left, the beginning of a small stream that crosses the road. At 3.1 miles and 3.4 miles, you pass short trails to the right, which lead to Lake Latini, visible in winter and early spring through the trees.

At 3.7 miles, leave the road at a culvert to turn left on a gravel spur for a side trip to Table Rock. Through a hemlock ravine, Caledonia Creek can be heard rushing off to the left. At 3.9 miles, you reach Table Rock, a flat rock terrace approximately 200 by 500 feet. There is little plant growth through the small cracks on the surface of the rock. Scrub pine, oak, and juniper have made a few inroads along the edge of the rock. From a fence you can look down on a swampy area and the Fire Road. Warblers and vireos are attracted by a half dozen nesting boxes surrounding the flat rock.

Retrace your steps and rejoin the Fire Road at 4.1 miles. Boggy areas with skunk cabbage line both sides of the road just below Table Rock. Pass the turnoff for the AT, then Lake Lenape, and return to your car at 4.3 miles.

For more information, contact U.S. Department of the Interior, National Park Service, Delaware Water Gap National Recreation Area, Bushkill, PA 18324.

5. PENNEL RUN

Distance	7.2 miles
Elevation	650 feet
Time to hike	3½ hours
Surface	Rocky woods trail
Interesting features	Natural area
Facilities	None
Hunting	Yes

Directions

From I-84 (Exit 8) between Scranton and the New Jersey–New York line:

1. South on PA 402 for 14.3 miles to Snow Hill Road
2. Right onto Snow Hill Road (TR 317) for 2.3 miles to parking lot on right

Coordinates 41°09'54"N; 75°07'14"W

Pennel Run is in a wild, untamed section of the Delaware State Forest. The trail is very rocky, so wear your hiking boots. And keep your eyes open. We saw a very large black bear (it must have weighed 600 to 700 pounds) near the trail on our last visit here in May. The bear hardly seemed to notice us, though. He just continued into the woods.

The hike is part of the Thunder Swamp Trail System and has been recently blazed. To access the start, walk a few feet more on Snow Hill Road to the blue-blazed main trail marked by a hiking symbol. Head north past a trail register.

The trail gets rockier and a little slippery as you descend into a swampy area in a hemlock grove. Soon you climb up again, passing three old white pine trees at least 5 feet in diameter. Mostly the forest is composed of beech, oak, and hickory.

At .8 mile you cross 20-foot-wide Spruce Run on a well-built bridge. The water is reddish brown, tinged by tannin in the swamps it drains. You reach an intersection at 1.6 miles. The blue-blazed main Thunder Swamp Trail turns right. You turn left, following the red-blazed side trail to the Pennel Run Natural Area. The trail continues rocky, but drier.

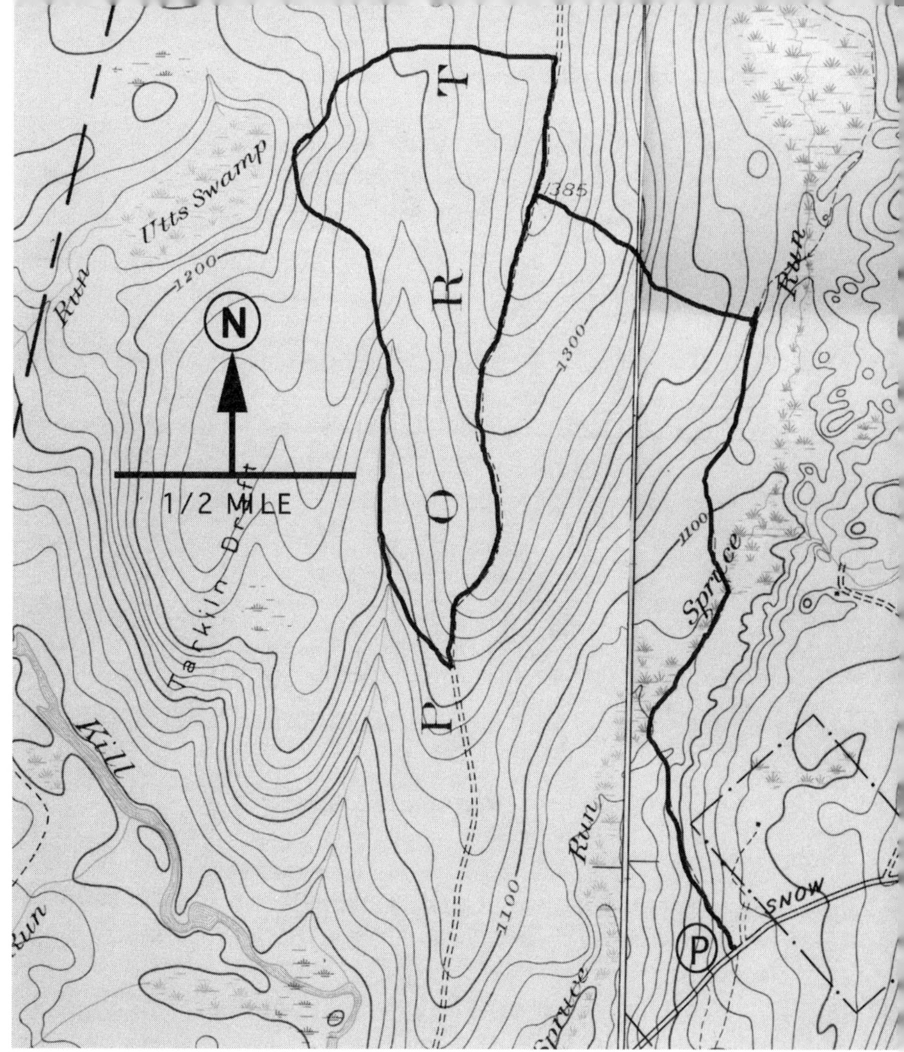

At 2.1 miles, turn right on an old fire road—Hay Road, the beginning of the Pennel Run Loop. In another five to eight minutes (.2 mile), watch closely for the double red blazes and turn left, leaving the road.

The trail leads down to the edge of Utts Swamp. Red efts, the terrestrial stage of the red-spotted newt, are bright orange here. In nearby swamps, they vary in color from brown to red.

There are many intersecting trails here. Watch carefully for double blazes, indicating turns. Highbush blueberries alternate

Red-spotted newt

with acres of ferns, with usually a sharp demarcation between the two. Ferns release chemicals into the soil that are toxic to competing vegetation.

At 4 miles, you cross slow-moving Pennel Run on mossy rocks and head steeply uphill. At 4.2 miles, reach Hay Road again and turn left. The road is straight and relatively rock free—a welcome change from the rough trail you just left. Follow a ridgeline for almost a mile of easy walking, then complete the Pennel Run Loop at 5.1 miles and turn right, retracing your steps.

There are more hiking opportunities in the Thunder Swamp System. See Hike No. 6. Contact the Delaware State Forest for more information.

6. STILLWATER NATURAL AREA

Distance	8.6 miles
Elevation	80 feet
Time to hike	4½ hours
Surface	Rocky woods trail, old road
Interesting features	Swamps, wildlife
Facilities	None
Hunting	Yes

Directions

From I-84 (Exit 8) between Scranton and the New Jersey–New York line:

1. South on PA 402 for 10.4 miles to Old Bushkill Road
2. Turn left on Old Bushkill Road (SR 2003) for 1.5 miles to Flat Ridge Road
3. Turn left on Flat Ridge Road for 2.1 miles, to a pull-off on the right

Coordinates 41°14'31"N; 75°01'40"W

This second hike in the Thunder Swamp Trail System contains swamps and many opportunities to see wildlife. From the parking lot, walk down a short rocky trail to Painter Swamp at a sign and trail register. Turn right on the red-blazed trail. You have excellent views into the swamp. There is plenty of evidence of beavers in the chewed and fallen logs and several lodges in the swamp.

The trail is a foot or so higher than swamp level in a hardwood forest, which includes oak, maple, and birch. We found a fine example of sulfur shelf, a dramatic layered shelf fungus, growing on an oak tree. The color was bright orange, with a yellow underside. Beavers have raised the level of the swamp, and there is open water on the far side. Spatterdock, with yellow flowers in June, and white water lilies cover the slow-moving near side.

Turn left at a sign for the Stillwater Natural Area. At .7 mile, cross Painter Creek on logs over a beaver dam. The trail is partially flooded; red blazes are visible on rocks in the water.

Bear right at a trail intersection, then continue ahead up a woods road, watching carefully for double red blazes. After 50 feet on the road, the trail turns right into the woods. Double red blazes are

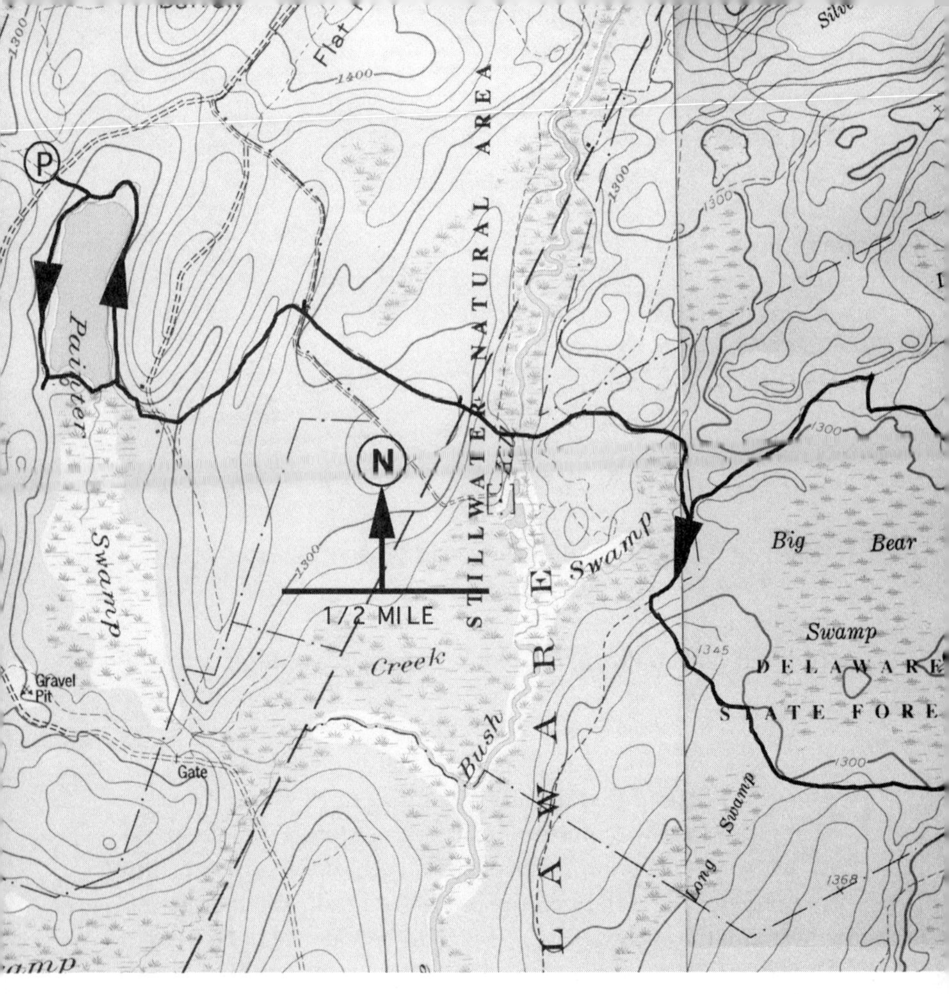

painted on a tree and a rock in the trail, which was covered with dirt and grass when we were last there.

There are several intersecting roads and trails in this area. Watch carefully for the red blazes. At .9 mile, you reach another sign for the Stillwater Natural Area. Turn left on the blue-blazed main trail of the Thunder Swamp System.

The trail continues south, but again, watch carefully for turns. A double pile of rocks in the middle of the trail indicates a 90-degree turn to the left (east). Reach Coon Swamp Road at 1.4 miles at a sign for Big Bear Swamp 1 mile ahead.

The red-blazed North, or Flat Ridge, Loop turns left up Coon Swamp Road. This loop would add 3.3 miles to your hike, but it cannot be recommended, as it is poorly maintained once you leave Coon Swamp Road and all but disappears in the swamp near the "stillwaters" of Little Bushkill Creek.

Continue ahead, crossing the road on the blue-blazed trail. Pass another trail register. At 1.8 miles, the North Loop Trail comes in from the left. Continue ahead on the blue-blazed trail.

Cross a bridge over Little Bushkill Creek, where mountain laurel is in bloom in early June. The trail descends from a rocky ledge. Turn left at a trail intersection, then step across a small stream at a sign for the Big Bear Loop. At 2.4 miles, you reach a T intersection at a woods road. Turn right for the Big Bear Loop.

The outlet for Big Bear Swamp crosses the old woods road. Cross either on rocks or on a bridge 50 feet downstream. The road becomes a rough trail as you skirt the swamp.

Climb up the first of many layered rock ledges. There's a good chance you might pick up ticks as you brush up against highbush

Rhododendron

blueberries, which at times obscure the trail. Blueberries alternate with royal fern, 3 feet high, which also makes it hard to see the rocks in the trail.

There is not as much standing water here as at Painter Swamp. Thick black spruce, white pine, and dense rhododendron prevent views into the swamp. There are many birds, including warblers and vireos. Cross a slow-moving stream on a log bridge. Reach the road you were on to start the loop and turn left, following blue blazes.

At 6 miles, complete Big Bear Loop and turn right back on the blue-blazed trail, retracing your steps. At 7.5 miles, turn right on the red-blazed Painter Loop, on the east side of Painter Swamp. At 8.6 miles, you are at your car.

7. BLOOMING GROVE 4-H TRAIL

Distance	4.6 miles
Elevation	260 feet
Time to hike	2½ hours
Surface	Rocky trail, grassy road
Interesting features	Wooded swamp, tannic stream
Facilities	None
Hunting	Yes

Directions

From I-84 (Exit 8) between Scranton and the New Jersey–New York line:

1. North on PA 402 for 3.9 miles
2. Turn left at the Blooming Grove Hiking Trail sign at the parking lot

Coordinates 41°24'59"N; 75°08'26"W

Remember your hiking boots and insect repellent for this interesting hike in the Delaware State Forest. The trail is quite rocky through swamp and woodland and includes several small stream crossings. Also, take a pail if you like berries. Blueberries prefer the acidic soil at the edge of the swamp and ripen in July and August. Wild strawberries are ready in June, and red raspberries in July; both prefer the sunny power-line cut. Built by the local 4-H Club in 1975, the trail has been blazed recently and is well maintained by volunteers. Begin walking from the parking lot through a grassy power-line cut to a large sign indicating the trail system of three loops.

Within a few hundred feet, bear right on the red-blazed Blue Heron Swamp Trail through mixed oaks and birches. The path is very rocky and often wet, crossing an intermittent stream on logs. Swamp wildflowers, including violets and golden thread, thrive in the moist and acidic soil. You can catch glimpses of the Blue Heron Swamp on your left through the trees. A closer view of the swamp and its inhabitants can be found farther along the hike.

At .5 mile, turn right on the white-blazed White Deer Trail; then at .9 mile, bear left on the blue-blazed Gates Meadow Loop. Cross two intermittent streams on stepping-stones. When you reach the

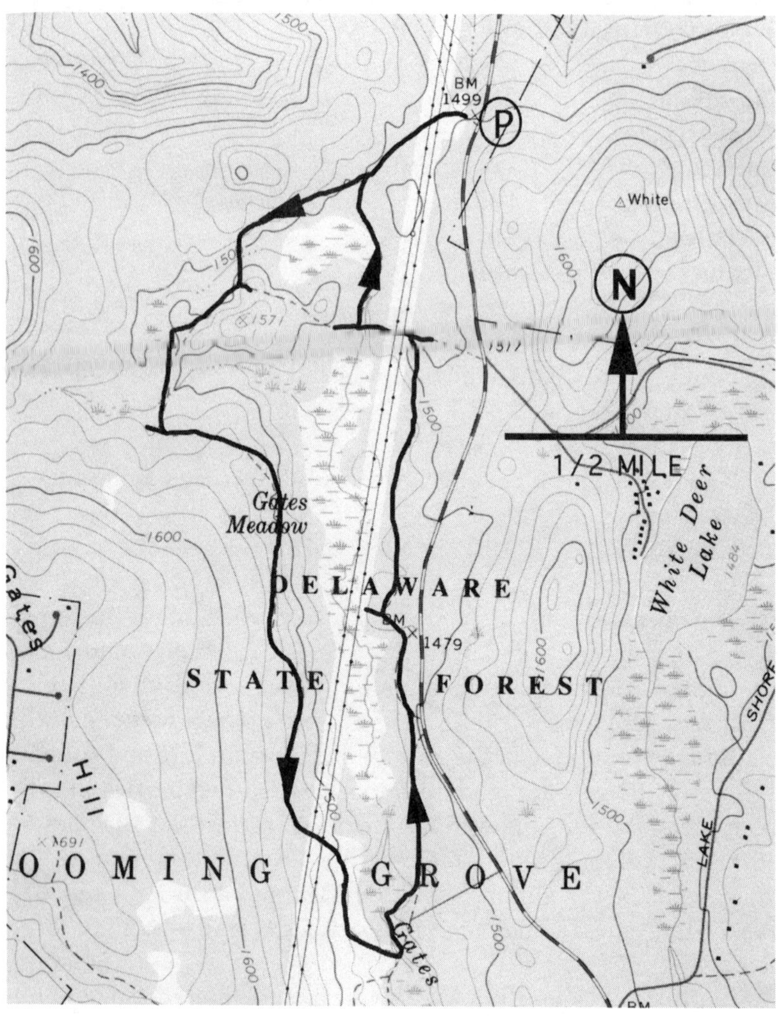

power-line cut again, look for wild strawberries and raspberries in the open grassy field. Blue arrows on the rocks point the way to reenter the woods.

At 2.3 miles, reach Gates Run, a 15-foot-wide tannin-filled stream. Tea-colored water tumbles over rocks through mature hemlocks. Tannin is produced by sphagnum moss and acid-loving plants in the swamp, which is drained by the stream. It is unusual to find this much tannin in a free-flowing stream. Dense shade and the acidic soil created by the tannin discourage any undergrowth. Turn right to walk downstream.

Shortly, you turn left at a field reverting to woods, then left again on a grassy road. Cross Gates Run on a culvert. Watch carefully for the double blue blazes indicating a left turn opposite a small cabin. Walk along Gates Run until you reach another set of double blue blazes; then turn right, away from the stream.

The trail turns left on a grassy road, a light blue carpet of bluets in May, then adjoins PA 402 very briefly. Several large boulders invite a rest stop. Turn left back into woods on another grassy road. Shortly, the trail leads uphill, the only steep climb of this hike.

At 3.8 miles, the blue trail ends. Turn left on the white trail and cross the power-line cut again, another chance to pick strawberries and raspberries in the summer. Reenter the woods, and at 4 miles, cross Gates Run. Almost immediately, turn right on the red-blazed Blue Heron Swamp Trail.

Jack-in-the-pulpit

This area affords the closest view of the swamp as you skirt the edge, stepping on moss- and lichen-covered rocks and logs. White ash, swamp oak, red maple, and swamp azalea grow along the fringe of the swamp; skunk cabbage, jack-in-the-pulpit, and ferns are common ground plants. Dense thickets and vegetation provide cover for many animals and keep you on the trail. Beavers have created an area of open water in the middle of the swamp. You are likely to see a hawk perching in the branches of a skeletal tree searching for prey, and hear woodpeckers drilling for grubs in the decaying wood. Herons, grebes, and mallards find nesting sites at the edge of the swamp. Smaller swamp dwellers include wood frogs, salamanders, spring peepers, and garter and ribbon snakes. And of course, there are plenty of mosquitoes, gnats, and ticks.

At 4.5 miles, you complete the red loop. Cross the power-line cut and retrace your steps to your car.

8. BRUCE LAKE NATURAL AREA

Distance	8 miles
Elevation	220 feet
Time to hike	3¾ hours
Surface	Rocky trails, woods road, several stream crossings
Interesting features	Glacial and artificial lakes, swamps, wildlife, blueberries
Facilities	None
Hunting	Yes

Directions

From I-84 (Exit 7) between Scranton and the New Jersey–New York line: south on PA 390 for .1 mile to Bruce Lake Natural Area parking area on the left

Coordinates 41°21'44"N; 75°12'04"W

This hike includes two lakes—one glacial and the other man-made—and several swamps on a typical Pocono rocky trail in the Delaware State Forest. The trail is blue-blazed throughout. As we describe it, you take the longest route through Bruce Lake Natural Area. To shorten the hike, make a series of right turns at trail intersections.

Begin by walking around the yellow metal gate on the blue-blazed Egypt Meadow Trail. There is a trail register here. Turn right on Panther Swamp Road at .2 mile; shortly, turn left on an extremely rocky trail that follows the edge of Egypt Meadow Lake.

Egypt Meadow Lake is a shallow, artificial lake of 60 acres constructed in 1935 by the Civilian Conservation Corps. The water has a brownish tinge, due to the adjacent 100-acre Balsam Swamp. Early on a May morning, the lake was as placid and reflective as a mirror, disturbed only by a mallard family paddling along the shore.

Turn left at Bruce Lake Road, then cross a wooden bridge over the end of the lake—the lake inlet and Balsam Swamp are on your right. The trail leads gradually uphill. Notice the large rock outcropping on your left, 20 feet high and several hundred feet long. Rock layers and boulders are favorite places for bears to den. This is indeed prime bear habitat, and we saw plenty of signs here—tracks

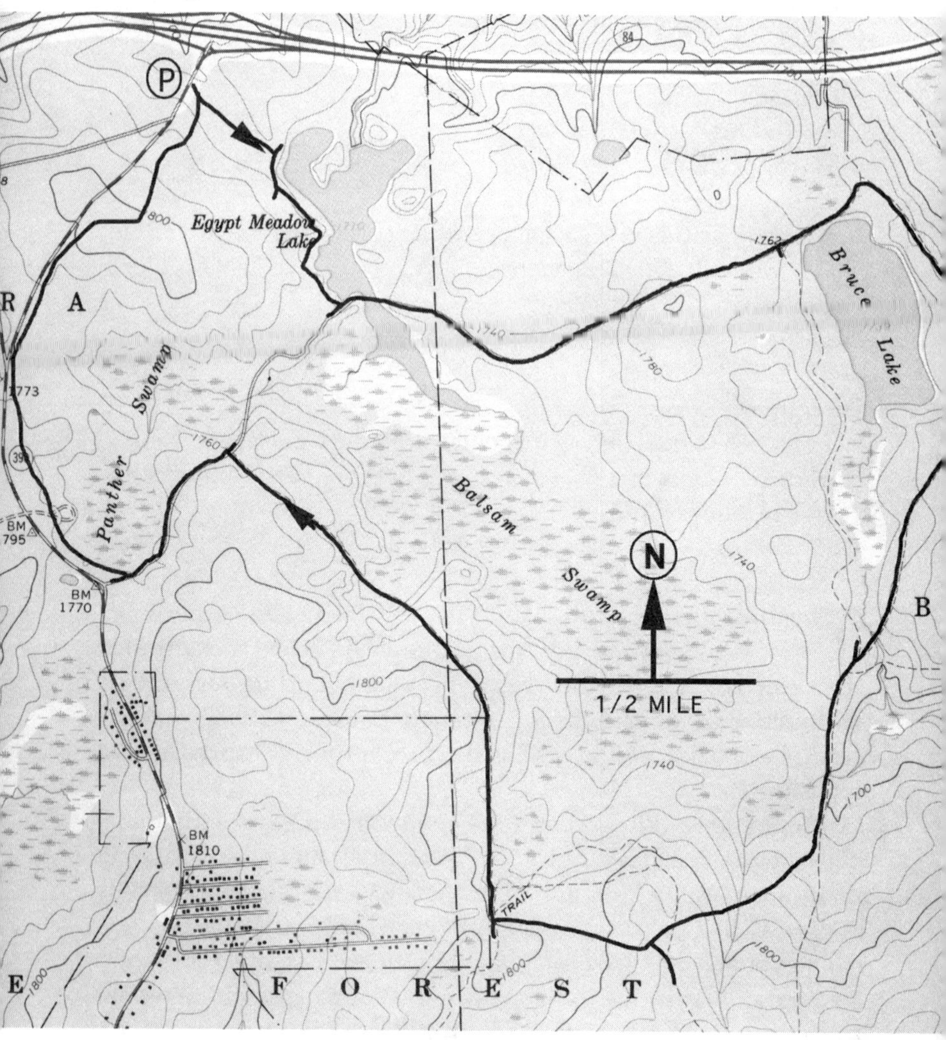

in the mud, scat, scratches on trees, and rocks overturned in the bear's search for grubs. We do not recommend you make any special effort to walk quietly through these woods. Bears are generally reclusive and avoid humans, but they do not like to be surprised.

At 2 miles, you reach an intersection with the West Branch Bruce Lake Trail. Continue straight ahead. At 2.5 miles, the road continues ahead, but you turn right, following the blue blazes on a trail with a sign reading, "More Difficult."

There is an expanse of highbush blueberries as far as the eye can see as you round the northern end of Bruce Lake. The blueberries are large, their color is medium to light blue, they are not seedy, and they ripen in late summer. They are easy to pick at waist level and above. In contrast, huckleberries ripen earlier, are low to the ground, are purple to black in color, and are seedy.

Bruce Lake is a pristine glacial lake covering 48 acres, with an average depth of 7 feet and a maximum depth of 20 feet. In contrast to the dark tannic water of Egypt Meadow Lake, Bruce Lake is blue-green, indicating algae. The lake is fed entirely by groundwater and is drained by Shohola Creek. The rocky, poorly drained soil near the lake discourages the growth of larger trees. Plenty of light filters through to encourage thick stands of blueberries and sheep and mountain laurel.

Cross a bridge over Shohola Creek. At a trail intersection, turn left on the Bruce Lake Trail. Blueberries and laurel give way to ferns in wetter areas in the open woodland.

At 3 miles, you again descend a slope toward Shohola Creek. Beavers have dammed the creek and created a very wet meadow. Cross marshy areas, then the creek on stepping-stones. Along the stream, hemlock and rhododendron again predominate.

After a 180-foot climb through mixed oak forest, turn right on the Rock Oak Ridge Trail at 4 miles. In another .5 mile, turn right on the Brown Trail. The trail follows the wire-fenced boundary of the village of Promised Land on your left for a short distance. The 100-acre Balsam Swamp is on your right, but your view into the swamp is obscured by thick stands of rhododendron and laurel. The rhododendron blooms in July, the laurel in June.

At 6 miles, turn left for easy walking on Bruce Lake Road. Panther Swamp is on your right. There are no panthers left, but you may see bobcat, coyote, or fox tracks. Just before the yellow metal gate at PA 390, turn right on the Snowshoe Trail. The walking is easy on a cross-country ski trail through mature oaks. You are likely to spot turkeys feeding on the acorns. Turn left at Egypt Meadow Trail to return to the parking lot and your car.

9. SHUMAN POINT NATURAL AREA

Distance	3 miles
Elevation	240 feet
Time to hike	1¼ hours
Surface	Rocky trail, old roads
Interesting features	Lake Wallenpaupack
Facilities	None
Hunting	Yes

Directions

From I-84 (Exit 6) between Scranton and the New Jersey–New York line:

1. North on PA 507 for 12.5 miles to US 6
2. Turn left (west) on US 6 for 1.3 miles to PA 590
3. Turn left (west) on PA 590 for 2 miles to a parking lot on the left

Coordinates 41°26'54"N; 75°12'28"W

Lake Wallenpaupack, 13 miles long, is the largest impoundment of water in the Poconos. Built by the Pennsylvania Power and Light Company in 1926 for the generation of hydroelectric power, the dam now serves only as an auxiliary power source. The main economic importance of the "Big Lake" today is its scenic and recreational value. The 250-acre Shuman Point is one of the few remaining wild areas adjoining Lake Wallenpaupack.

The walk to Shuman Point begins at the south end of the parking lot and heads uphill on a rocky, blue-blazed trail. The woods are composed of the mixed hardwoods, blueberries, and chestnut oaks typical of the Poconos. Also notice sprouts of American chestnuts from old stumps. At .2 mile, reach the top of a rocky knoll past a stand of white pine, with a view overlooking the woods toward the lake. Continue on the blue-blazed trail heading southwest.

At 1 mile, reach the edge of the lake on a grassy woods road. This road continues right into the water; in fact, it was the highway to the village of Wilsonville, inundated when the lake was built in 1926. There is still an area along PA 507 that the locals call Wilsonville.

The trail parallels the lake. Buttonbush, azalea, and willow grow along the lake edge. The water level varies during the season, so

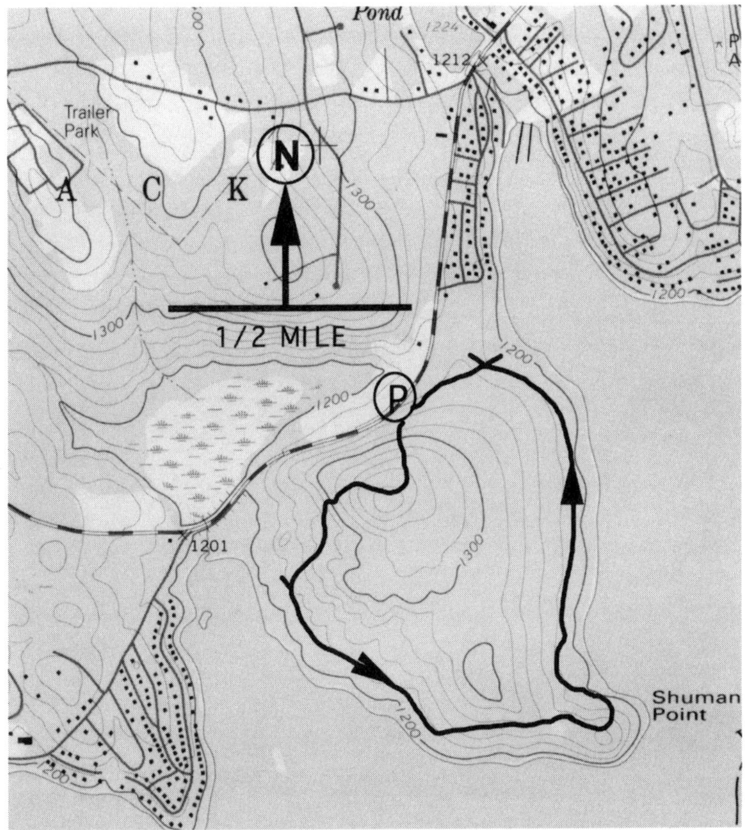

plants do not root in the water. Follow the blue blazes toward the end of Shuman Point, where a white pine tree grows in a clearing. This is an area of former farmers' fields, now overgrown with small hardwood saplings.

At 1.7 miles, reach a fork in the trail near a stone row fence. The Poconos are crisscrossed with these stone rows. Farmers piled the stones along the edges of their fields to get them out of the way and to enclose livestock. However, these "Pocono potatoes" stymied their best agricultural efforts, and farming proved unprofitable. Eventually, trees grew right in the middle of the fences, sprouting from nuts and acorns hidden there by squirrels. These trees, primarily deep-rooted oaks, are larger and older than the surrounding second-growth woods, mostly maples, that now grow in the abandoned fields. Walk through three additional breaks in the stone rows, which continue right into the water. The trail continues north along the edge of the lake on a woods road through pin oak, gray birch, and aspen.

Turn left (west) away from the lake on another old road at 2.4 miles. Notice two very old white pine trees. At 3 miles, you reach a wooden gate to the parking lot and your car.

The Beech House Creek Wildlife Refuge lies .5 mile farther west on the other side of PA 590. The refuge consists of 60 acres of wetlands, habitat for beavers, mallards, wood ducks, great blue herons, hawks, minks, raccoons, and otters. There are no trails through the Beech House Creek Refuge.

10. PROMISED LAND STATE PARK

Distance	3 miles
Elevation	173 feet
Time to hike	1¼ hours
Surface	Grassy road, rocky woods trail
Interesting features	Swamp, wildlife
Facilities	None
Hunting	Yes

Directions

From I-84 (Exit 7) between Scranton and the New Jersey–New York line: south on PA 390 for 1.3 miles to Kleinhans Trailhead parking lot on the right

Coordinates 41°20'37"N; 75°12'48"W

Promised Land was named in 1878 by optimistic settlers of the Shaker religious sect, who thought they had found a land of milk and honey. Instead, they found a land of rocks and swamps, unsuitable for farming or even gardening. They moved on, derisively calling the area "the promised land." You will enjoy the area more than the Shakers did. The rocks and swamps of Promised Land, at the northern edge of the Pocono plateau, are interesting geologically and are home to bears, deer, turkeys, and bobcats.

The Kleinhans Trail was recently blue-blazed and is easy to follow. Walk past a yellow metal gate and a trail register. Turn right on a grassy road with thick stands of paper birch, then maple and oak saplings. There are plenty of huckleberries to pick alongside the trail in July. This second-growth woods may have been the site of early farming efforts.

Soon you enter a hemlock and rhododendron forest to walk beside a small stream. At .8 mile, turn left on a woods road, staying on the blue-blazed trail. The road is rocky and wet, a favorite habitat for the red eft. Promised Land, and many other Pocono locations, is home to the eft—the juvenile, terrestrial stage of the red-spotted newt. Their color ranges from brown to scarlet to an almost fluorescent orange, but in the same location they all tend to have the same color. In some years, you will find it difficult to avoid stepping on them, they are so numerous. In late summer, the newt turns olive

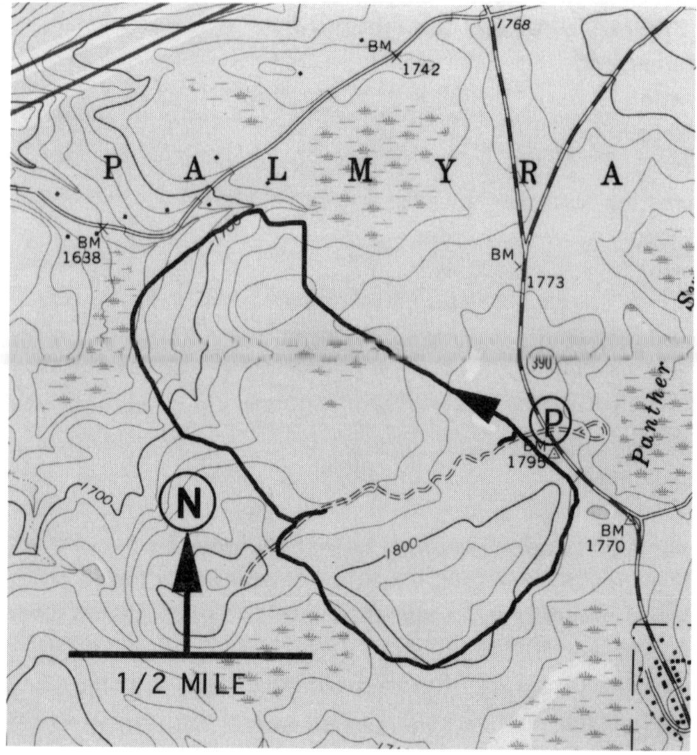

drab with a yellow underside with red spots and becomes completely aquatic, living and mating in shallow ponds.

Cross an intermittent stream, then a larger stream on a wooden bridge. At 1.6 miles, you reach an intersection with the Cross Cut Trail. (A left turn here leads .5 mile back to your car.) Continue straight ahead on the Kleinhans Trail.

Pass a large rock outcropping, then reach a sunny, grassy road. There are obvious signs of logging activity here, perhaps fifteen years ago. Scattered large stumps lie among the young birch, oak, maple, and beech. Turn left to reenter the mature forest at a yellow gate. At 3 miles, you reach the parking lot and your car.

There are several other interesting trails to explore in the 5,800-acre Promised Land State Park. Conservation Island Trail is a 1-mile nature trail on an island in the lake; the Little Falls Trail takes you past several waterfalls on the East Branch of Wallenpaupack Creek. Stop at the park office for a map of these and other trails.

11. TANNERSVILLE CRANBERRY BOG

Distance	1.5 miles
Elevation	50 feet
Time to hike	2 hours
Surface	Boardwalk and woodland trails
Interesting features	Unspoiled glacial bog, the southernmost low altitude boreal bog along the eastern seaboard
Facilities	Benches; no water or rest rooms
Hunting	No

Directions

From I-80 (Exit 45) west of Stroudsburg:
1. North on PA 715 for .5 mile to PA 611
2. Turn right (south) on PA 611 to Tannersville

A walk on the floating boardwalk through the Tannersville Cranberry Bog should not be missed. It is a fascinating place, a relic of the last glacial period over 13,000 years ago and a unique habitat for unusual plant and animal life. There are smaller bogs at higher elevations, but the Tannersville Bog, at 150 acres, is the largest in Pennsylvania.

Because of the fragility of the environment and the many rare species of plants and animals, a naturalist must accompany visitors to the bog on the Indian Ridge Boardwalk Trail. The Nature Conservancy owns the property, and a donation of $3 is requested ($2 for members of the Nature Conservancy). There are scheduled public walks on Sunday and Wednesday afternoons at 1:00. Reservations are suggested. Call 717-629-3061, or write Monroe County Conservation District, 8050 Running Valley Road, Stroudsburg, PA 18360, for a schedule of walks. Groups meet at the Monroe County Vo-Tech School, 1 mile north of Bartonsville on Laurel Lake Road.

A 1,700-foot boardwalk has been built across the bog from the oak-hickory and hemlock forest to slow-moving Cranberry Creek at the edge of the bog. A well-informed and helpful naturalist leads your small group on a two-hour walk, interpreting everything and answering all your questions. You will learn the unique features of a bog, fen, swamp, and marsh. And you will learn about the unusual flora and fauna found nowhere else but a bog.

As the naturalist explains, bog plants are derived from plant material and seeds brought in from higher latitudes by glaciation. The dominant plant is sphagnum moss, which forms a dense, floating mass on the water. Beneath the sphagnum, the water is cold and dark. The sphagnum produces tannin, which makes the water acidic and unfriendly to many plant species, including bacteria. Lacking drainage, the bog has gradually become darker and more acidic, with a pH of only 4.2. Nutrients such as nitrogen, calcium, and phosphorus are "locked up" in the vegetation instead of being recycled. As the sphagnum and other plants (as well as animals) die, they sink into the cold, acidic water and are preserved—sometimes for centuries (a woolly mammoth was found in a nearby bog). Gradually, the lake fills in with sphagnum, which decays as peat.

The trees of the bog send shallow root systems over the surface of the sphagnum and form unstable hummocks. They actually quake and sway when the wind blows or if someone jumps on the sphagnum mat nearby. These trees are far different from the adjoining hardwood forest. Black spruce and tamarack (American larch), normally found in Canada, predominate. The tamarack is the only deciduous northern conifer, losing its soft needles in October.

The bog is dominated by heath plants that can survive this hostile acidic environment—highbush blueberry, leatherleaf, sheep laurel, bog laurel, swamp azalea, and, of course, cranberry. Two others, bog rosemary and Labrador tea, are among Pennsylvania's rarer plants.

Insect-eating plants—the pitcher plant and the much smaller sundew plant—have adapted to the nutrient-poor soil conditions by luring, trapping, and digesting meals that have flown in. In the moist conditions of the bog, there are plenty of gnats and mosquitoes to dine on.

Unusual plants found nowhere else include orchids (several types), wild calla lily, cotton grass, rare yellow-eyed grass, and dwarf mistletoe, which grows as a parasite on the black spruce. In addition, there are many types of ferns, including cinnamon and royal, growing on the hummocks near the edge of the bog.

The bog also has its share of unusual and rare animal species, including black bears, coyotes, gray foxes, bobcats, wild turkeys, and barred owls. River otters, beavers, turtles, and green frogs are often

Black bear

seen at Cranberry Creek. Rarely seen are the bog turtle and the endangered bog copper butterfly. This butterfly lays its eggs only on the cranberry plant. Our naturalist said that she has yet to spot either a bog turtle or a bog butterfly. However, she did identify a buckbean (or bogbean), an aquatic, white, five-petaled flower—a species she had not seen here previously.

There is more hiking on the nearby North Woods and Fern Ridge Trails. See the section on nature trails.

12. BIG POCONO STATE PARK

Distance	5.6 miles
Elevation	1,566 feet
Time to hike	2½ hours
Surface	Rocky trail, grassy woods road
Interesting features	Views; wildlife, including black bears, timber rattlesnakes, deer; barrens-type vegetation
Facilities	Water, rest rooms, picnic tables, viewing telescopes at the parking lot
Hunting	Yes

Directions

From I-80 (Exit 45) west of Stroudsburg:

1. North on PA 715 for .2 mile to Sullivan Trail
2. Turn left onto Sullivan Trail (SR 4004) for 1 mile to Camelback Road
3. Turn left onto Camelback Road (SR 4006) for 4.3 miles to Big Pocono parking lot

Coordinates 41°02'36"N; 75°20'54"W

Tremendous views await the hiker at Big Pocono State Park from the top of Camelback Mountain. From an elevation of 2,132 feet at the edge of the Pocono Plateau, you have a fine view of the plateau to the north, the Delaware Water Gap to the southeast, and High Point, New Jersey, to the northeast. The Catskill Mountains of New York lie 84 miles to the northeast and are visible on a very clear day.

Vegetation, especially near the top, is of the barrens type. Note blueberries, currants, scrub pines, quaking aspens, and paper birches. Scrub pines, especially on exposed slopes, are shaped by the constant wind. The tallest scrub oaks and pines are only about 15 feet high at the summit. The elevation and the poor, shallow soil, consisting mostly of resistant sandstone, account for the sparse and stunted vegetation.

Park at the east end of the parking lot and begin hiking east downhill on a gravel path that leads through paper birch and mountain laurel. There are several intersecting trails here. Turn left at a

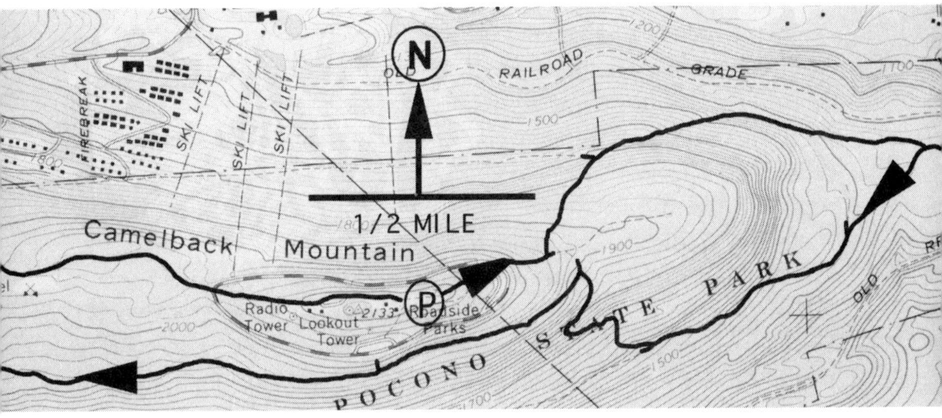

water fountain and continue downhill. At .3 mile, cross a parking lot and Rim Road, which circles the top of the mountain. A trail sign points the way to the North and South Trails. At .5 mile, turn left at a sign marking the North Trail.

The trail is not well marked but is easy to follow. Ski runs lie to your left just beyond the trees. North-side parklands are leased to the Camelback Ski Corporation. Funds from the resort and additional concessions from a restaurant at the top of the lifts provide all the revenue needed to operate the park. The eroded, rocky trail continues sharply downhill, as a mixed-oak forest replaces the scrubby growth of higher elevations. At 1 mile, the trail turns to the left at an unmarked intersection with a trail coming in from the right. A left turn (north) leads .2 mile to the Old RR Grade (blue-blazed) Trail. Instead, turn to the right (east) beside a field of blueberries. (Note: The park trail map is inaccurate in this area.) At 1.9 miles, pass an orange-blazed trail on the right identified as "Indian Trail." Continue straight ahead on the North Trail (concurrent with the Indian Trail on this stretch) on a grassy woods road.

At 2 miles, you reach a sign for the South Trail; turn right. The trail climbs steeply uphill but is relatively easy walking on a rocky woods road. The small to medium mixed hardwoods give way to paper birch and laurel as you ascend. At 3.2 miles, reach a trail intersection. The trail to the right would return you to the parking lot. Instead, turn left, staying on the South Trail. This trail is not well blazed either, although you may see a few faded yellow blazes.

Continue straight ahead on the South Trail, a very pretty section of the hike. This section of the trail is quite level, with great views to the south through the sparse and stunted vegetation. In June, the pink mountain laurel is spectacular against the white bark of birches. The blueberries here ripen in August, as opposed to July at lower elevations. At 3.6 miles, pass a sign on the right for the Vista Trail, which leads .1 mile to the parking lot.

At 4.6 miles, reach an intersection with an old woods road. A left turn would take you into State Game Lands 38 (see Hike No. 14). Instead, turn right. At 4.7 miles, walk around a yellow gate and turn right onto Camelback Road, walking on the left side, facing traffic. On the way back, pass the road to Cameltop, the leased restaurant concession operated by the Camelback Ski Corporation. Enter the park past a yellow metal gate. Pass the H. B. Rowland Heliport and the Big Pocono Fire Tower (elevation 2,131 feet). The fire tower was erected in 1921 and dedicated as a national historic fire tower in 1993. Both the fire tower and the heliport are operated by the Bureau of Forestry for the aircraft-assisted fire-suppression program and are staffed only during the spring and fall fire seasons.

Just before the parking lot, notice the small abandoned building. The stone cabin was built in 1908 by Henry S. Cattell, the former property owner, and was left unlocked for many years to be used as a shelter by anyone who wished. The Cattell cabin later served as a park office and nature museum. Big Pocono State Park is now operated by Tobyhanna State Park, and the small building is no longer used. At 5.6 miles, return to your car.

Big Pocono State Park is closed during the winter because of weather conditions. If you plan to hike in early spring, contact Tobyhanna State Park at 717-894-8336 to make sure it has reopened.

13. DEVIL'S HOLE

Distance	3 miles
Elevation	330 feet
Time to hike	2 ¼ hours
Surface	Rocky woods trail (which fades out the after first mile), many stream crossings
Interesting features	Box canyon, Devil's Hole, carved by a waterfall on Devil's Hole Creek
Facilities	None
Hunting	Yes

Directions

From I-380 (Exit 8) west of Stroudsburg:

1. East on PA 940 for 3.4 miles to Devil's Hole Road
2. Turn left (north) on Devil's Hole Road for 1.1 miles to parking area on left (at 90-degree bend in road)

Coordinates 41°08'30"N; 75°20'03"W

The difficulty in reaching Devil's Hole Creek Falls in State Game Lands 221, especially in spring and for the last half mile, practically guarantees solitude when you finally get there. Be prepared to wade across the stream, up to 2 feet deep during spring runoff, and to make your way through dense vegetation. From the game-lands parking lot, walk around a metal gate. As you descend to Devil's Hole Creek, mixed hardwoods give way to thick mountain laurel, which blooms in June.

You will cross the creek at least five times on your hike to Devil's Hole, and how wet you get will depend on recent rainfall. After heavy spring rains, we waded through water that was knee-deep. Later in the summer, you may be able to cross by stepping on rocks and logs without getting your feet wet.

At .8 mile you find a large stone barbecue, the remains of a retreat and hunting lodge built around the turn of the century by a former landowner named Thilenius, a wealthy New York food broker. An unusual grove of non-native tree species—majestic Norway spruce, fir, and cedar (red shaggy bark)—planted by the former owner surrounds the site.

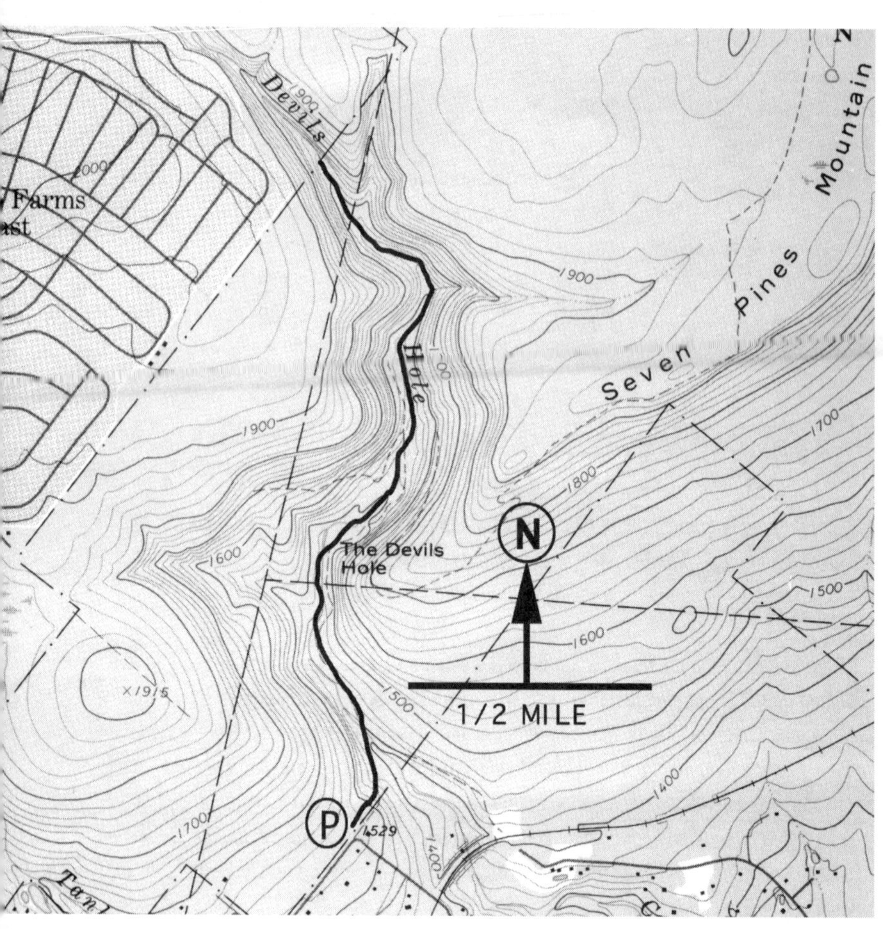

Just after the trees, notice more ruins on your right. It is rumored that the woodsy lodge was taken over in the 1920s for a combination still and speakeasy, which had a reputation for producing the finest moonshine around. Surprise raids by law enforcement would have been impossible at this secluded location. There is only one way in, along the stream, and lookouts could sound the warning in plenty of time for an escape.

Shortly, amid a stand of small maple saplings, notice a diversion channel along the stream lined with rocks. These ruins of the raceway are the only sign of a mill that once stood here. At 1 mile, pass another stone barbecue and cross Devil's Hole Creek to the east side.

From here, the trail becomes faint as you cling to rocks and rhododendron roots along the edge of the stream. You can, with difficulty, stay on the east side the rest of the way to Devil's Hole. Step across several mossy and fern-covered islands and streams as they flow into the creek from the right. The canyon walls, covered with rocks and rhododendron (blooms in July), become steeper and seem to close in. Then, just after the stream bends right 90 degrees to the northeast, you reach the falls. Devil's Hole is a large pothole carved out by the 25-foot cascade waterfall and, according to local legend, has limitless depth. Several flat boulders at the base of the falls present an inviting place for a rest. The pool looks like a nice place for a swim, but keep in mind that the water is very deep and the surrounding rocks are slippery.

Backtrack to your last stream crossing, opposite the second stone barbecue. You can hike up steep stone steps and then follow an old woods road east out of the gorge for some interesting hiking along the top of Seven Pines Mountain. However, to return to your car without crossing private property, you must follow the creek back out to the parking lot.

14. WOLF SWAMP AND DEEP LAKE

Distance	4.2 miles
Elevation	540 feet
Time to hike	2 hours
Surface	Rough woods road, abandoned railroad grade, power-line cut
Interesting features	Pennsylvania kettle lakes, boulder field
Facilities	None
Hunting	Yes

Directions

From I-80 (Exit 45) west of Stroudsburg:

1. North on PA 715 for .2 mile to Sullivan Trail
2. Turn left onto Sullivan Trail (SR 4004; follow signs to Camelback) for 1 mile to Camelback Road
3. Turn left onto Camelback Road (SR 4006) for 3.1 miles to State Game Lands 38 parking lot on the right

Coordinates 41°02'47"N; 75°22'28"W

State Game Lands 38 contains 3,943 acres of forest adjacent to Big Pocono State Park and is undeveloped, with rocky, little-used roads and an abandoned railroad grade. A boulder field and kettle lakes are reminders of glacial history. The glacier gouged out depressions, which filled with melting ice. These lakes are fed by groundwater alone and, on a geologic scale, are temporary features. They will eventually fill with sediment and become swamp and then forest.

Begin by walking west around a metal gate uphill on the Viper Trail, on a gravel and dirt road; you immediately pass your return route at a power-line road on your right. At .1 mile, walk under a power line and pass a microwave tower on your right, then a forest of five more towers on your left. From here, the road is closed to traffic and is fairly rough.

At .2 mile, turn right (north) on a red gravel road. You immediately pass a 200-by-200-foot boulder field on your left. The vegetation is the typical "barrens" type, including laurel, leatherleaf, blueberry, scrub oak, and scrub pine. Wild azalea blooms in May, laurel in June. At .4 mile, the road bears left (west).

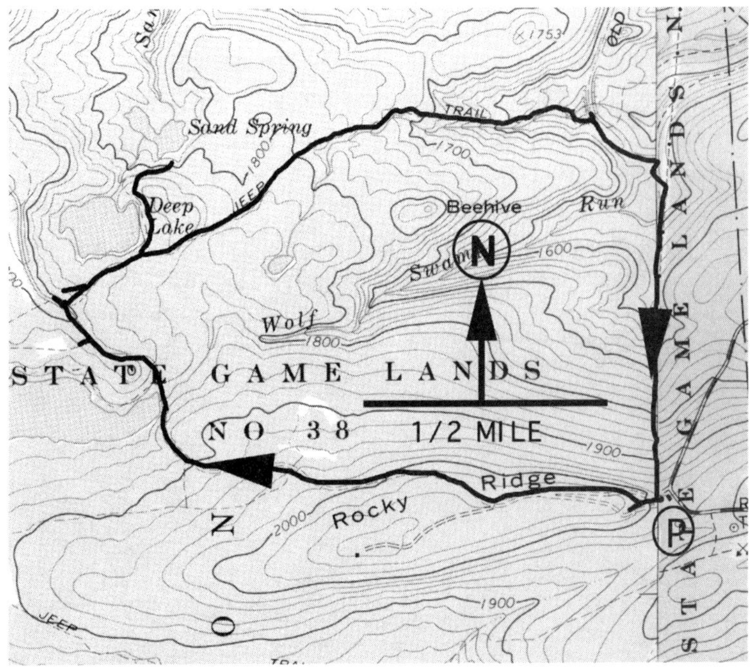

A sign painted on a large boulder at .5 mile indicates a right turn for Wolf Swamp and Deep Lake. Pass an abandoned quarry for the red gravel used to build the road. Follow this road north and reach Wolf Swamp at 1.2 miles. Walk across an earthen dam; the swamp and lake, with skeletal trees, is to your left. Wolf Swamp Run drains the shallow lake.

Continue across the impoundment. At 1.3 miles, a road comes in from the left. Continue ahead, turning right at the next two trail intersections.

Deep Lake is soon visible to your left through the trees. Several trails lead down to the lovely circular lake. Continue straight ahead on the grassy woods road. At 1.5 miles, a grassy wide trail comes in from the left (a turn here ends at Sand Spring Lake, another glacial lake, for a .6-mile round-trip).

Continue straight ahead on a rocky road, downhill through woods filled with mountain and sheep laurel and rhododendron. Mountain laurel blooms white and pink in June. Sheep laurel also flowers in June but is lower to the ground, and the blooms are a darker pink. Rhododendron prefers lower elevations and blooms in July.

Cross a stream over a culvert. At 2.7 miles, turn right on an old railroad grade, an abandoned line of the Wilkes-Barre and Eastern Railroad. Soon the railbed is elevated 80 to 100 feet above the surrounding oak-hickory forest. Look down to your right on yet another glacial pond. At 3 miles, turn right on a woods road, which soon opens up to a power-line cut. Turn right, following the steep road uphill. Strawberries and blueberries are found at the open power-line cut. At 4.2 miles, turn left on the road you walked in on to return to your car.

15. TOBYHANNA STATE PARK

Distance	5.1 miles
Elevation	80 feet
Time to hike	2½ hours
Surface	Improved base of crushed stone and gravel
Interesting features	5,440 acres of woodland and swamps, 170-acre lake
Facilities	Water, picnic facilities at the boat launch and beach areas; rest rooms at beach area
Hunting	No

Directions

From I-380 (Exit 7) east of Wilkes-Barre:

1. South on PA 611 for .3 mile to PA 423
2. Turn left (north) on PA 423 for 4.4 miles (through Tobyhanna) to Park Road
3. Turn left on Park Road for .6 mile to parking area 5 on the right

Coordinates 41°13'02"N; 75°24'20"W

Tobyhanna is an Indian word meaning "a stream whose banks are fringed with alder." Tobyhanna Lake, too, is fringed with alder and willows. Tobyhanna (and also nearby Gouldsboro and Klondike Lakes) was created for the ice-harvesting industry. Ice was cut from these lakes in winter and stored in large insulated buildings. During the summers from 1900 to 1936, up to 150 boxcar loads per day were shipped out of these lakes to eastern cities and as far south as Florida.

The Lakeside Trail at Tobyhanna, which circles the lake, is especially suited to families with young children or older persons, including the physically challenged. The trail passes through many of the varied habitats found in northeastern Pennsylvania, including a mixed hardwood forest of oak, beech, birch, and maple; a swamp; a hemlock-spruce forest; and the lake. We hiked here after a March snowfall and found only the tracks of four-legged trail users: bobcat, rabbit, beaver, and bear.

The trail begins at the northwest edge of the parking lot. Walk past a yellow metal gate, slightly uphill on a gravel road. The trail is

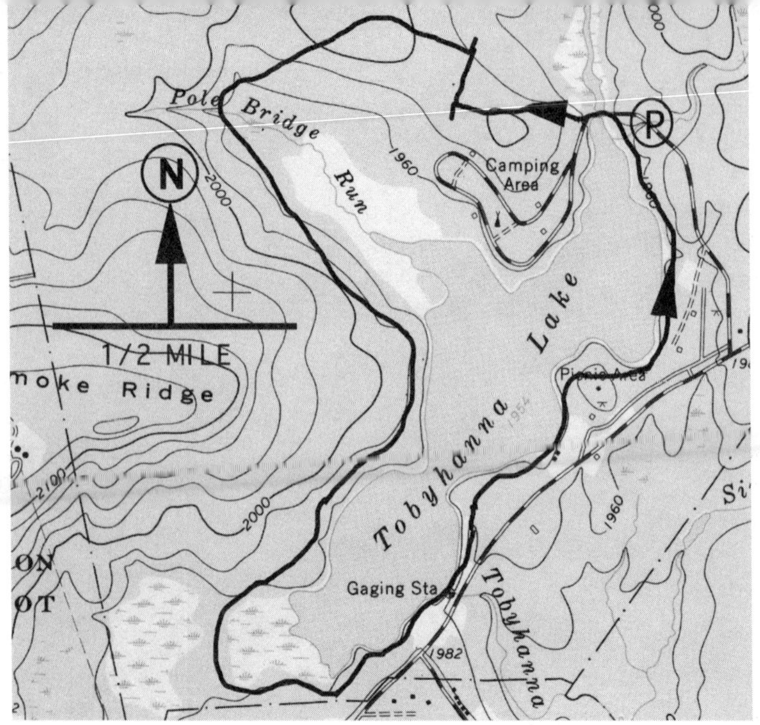

well blazed with light blue on the trees and some rocks. At .2 mile, you reach a trail intersection. Turn right, following the arrows, for the Lakeside Trail.

There is no sign of the lake yet through a mixed hardwood forest. At .5 mile, a yellow-blazed trail continues straight ahead. Bear to the left, following the blue blazes. There are occasional swampy areas to either side, with mosses, ferns, and blueberries. Off to the right, Black Bear Swamp contains habitat for deer and snakes, as well as bears.

At 1 mile, you reach the trailhead for the Frank Gantz Trail, a rocky and demanding 3.3-mile hike linking Tobyhanna with Gouldsboro State Park and its trail system. Continue straight ahead on the Lakeside Trail. At 1.2 miles, a culvert crosses Pole Bridge Run. Shortly afterward you have your first glimpse of the lake through the trees, but then you veer away from it again.

After crossing another stream at 2.3 miles, you enter a shady hemlock-spruce and rhododendron forest. At 2.7 miles, as you approach the lake again, the vegetation gives way to graceful clumps of paper birches and more blueberries. Reach a parking lot, the dam, and PA 423 at 3 miles. Signs warn against walking across the 20-foot dam. Instead, walk down and cross the 60-foot-wide Tobyhanna Creek below the dam on a bridge. The water is reddish black from the tannin content.

On the other side, look for blue blazes on the trees at the edge of the woods. There is a steep grassy embankment up to the lake that levels off and is easily ascended. Ducks and geese raise their families near the dam and will probably object if you venture too close in the spring.

At 3.5 miles, reach a boat rental and launch area, with water and picnic facilities. At 4 miles, you come to a swimming beach and rest rooms. Beavers have taken down many smaller beech and willow trees and have gnawed quite vigorously on many others. At 4.8 miles, the trail veers off to the right away from the lake. At 5 miles, you reach the paved road, still following the blue blazes. Turn left, crossing the slow-moving Tobyhanna Creek. The parking lot is just to your right along the creek.

Bobcat

16. GOULDSBORO STATE PARK

Distance	5.7 miles
Elevation	350 feet
Time to hike	3 hours
Surface	Very rocky path, worn concrete/asphalt road
Interesting features	2,800-acre park, with 250-acre lake
Facilities	Rest rooms, picnic tables, grills, water at the lakeside picnic area
Hunting	Yes

Directions

From I-380 (Exit 6) east of Wilkes-Barre:

1. North on PA 507 for 2.1 miles to State Park Road
2. Turn right on State Park Road (park entrance) for .9 mile
3. Turn left at parking lot 1 for .2 mile to parking area

Coordinates 41°14'07"N; 75°27'25"W

The town of Gouldsboro and this park were named for Jay Gould, described unflatteringly on commemorative road signs as a "noted speculator and railroad manipulator" with far-flung interests. For his first business venture, from 1856 to 1861, he owned a large tannery in nearby Thornhurst.

Begin the hike at the parking lot beside a park sign. Light blue blazes mark the Prospect Rock Trail on an old woods road, formerly a campsite road. This park was once open for overnight camping but is now strictly for day use, including swimming, boating, and fishing in the summer and ice fishing in the winter.

Double blue blazes indicate a left turn, off the woods road onto a rocky path. At .9 mile, you reach State Park Road. Cross the road and turn right facing traffic, following the blue blazes painted on the guardrail. You pass a swamp on the left, with skeletal trees. Watch carefully for a turn to the left at 1.1 miles to continue through the woods on a rough and rocky trail.

You are on the edge of the park property, and several private homes are visible through the trees to your right. Gradually you turn to the left, away from the houses. The trail ascends 150 feet on a boulder-strewn hillside to Prospect Rock. Reaching the top at 1.4 miles, the trail levels a bit but is still rocky.

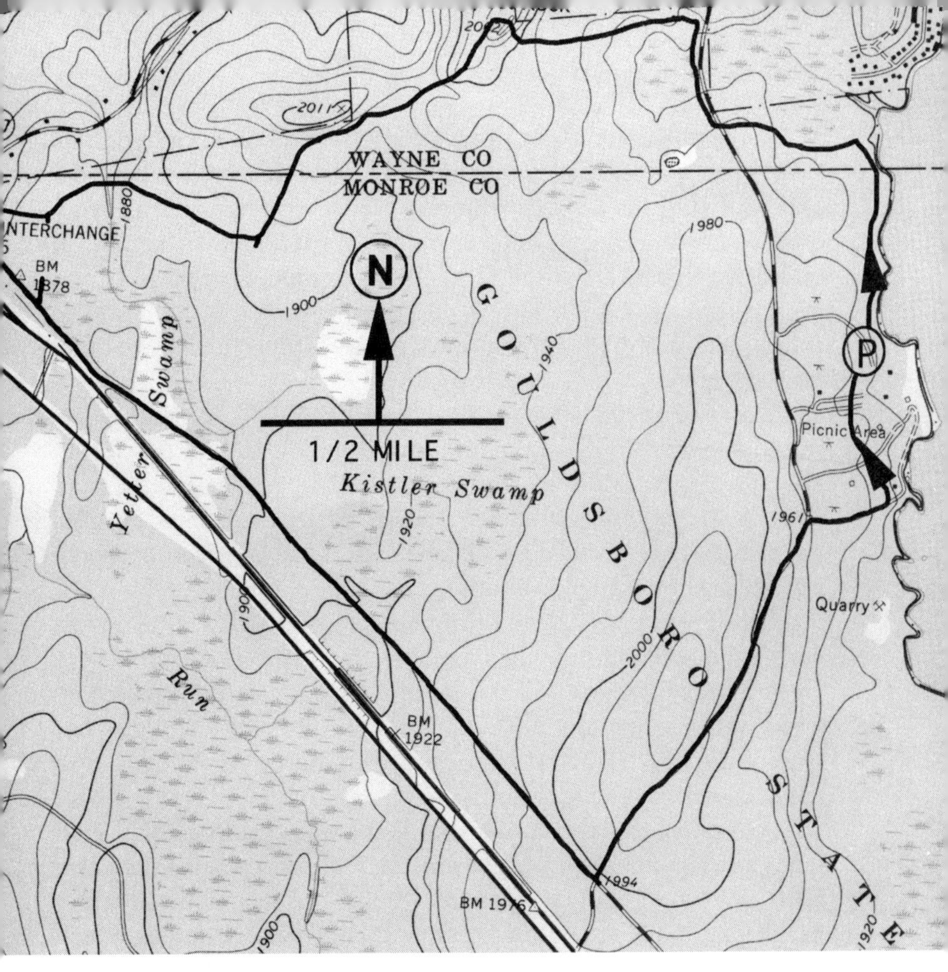

At 2 miles, I almost stepped on several baby chicks in the path, which scurried away beneath my feet. Immediately, and only 3 feet away, a large hen turkey stood up from behind a rock. She didn't move away but just stood and looked at us. In a moment, three more chicks scurried away in front of me. Thinking there were no more, I took a step forward and almost stepped on three or four more. Finally, their mother, after gathering her brood (twelve in all), slowly moved away, keeping a wary eye on us the whole time. Turkeys are increasingly abundant in Pennsylvania woods. They like mast, especially acorns, hickory nuts, and beechnuts, so are likely to be found in hardwood forests. They also like the clover, grasses, and insects found at field edges. Weighing up to 25 pounds, turkeys can fly but prefer to stay on the ground.

At 2.2 miles, you come to a trail intersection. Turn right on the clearly marked trail, following the blue blazes. At 2.3 miles, the blue blazes turn to the left at a trail sign for the Connector Trail (you could follow the blue-blazed trail to Old PA 611 for a total hike of 5.3 miles). For this hike, continue straight ahead on the red-blazed Connector Trail. At 2.4 miles, you step over a reddish black (tannin-colored) 10-foot-wide stream on stepping-stones and through a hemlock grove.

Traffic noise tends to drown out birdsong briefly as you come to the edge of the woods at the intersection of PA 507 and the northbound exit ramp of I-380. At 2.5 miles you find an old concrete road (Old PA 611) that was abandoned when I-380 was built. Trees, grasses, and shrubs have invaded the concrete. The red blazes continue and are replaced by light blue blazes again.

Old PA 611 goes directly through Kistler Swamp, and you are surrounded on both sides by typical swamp vegetation and skeletal trees; a beaver lodge and a chorus of bullfrogs complete the scene. I-380 traffic is perhaps 500 feet off to the right. Although our feet were quite dry, it must have appeared to motorists as if we were actually walking in the swamp.

At 4 miles, you reenter a rock-filled hardwood forest. The trail leads steadily uphill and away from the road. Beech is the predominant tree throughout Gouldsboro, with an occasional hickory. This results in a more open forest canopy than in nearby forests, which are mostly oak. The lovely light gray bark of many of the beeches is scarred by beech scale infestation followed by bark canker. Striped maple (moosewood) and aspen are found at the woods edge. At 4.3 miles, turn left at an intersection with the abandoned park entrance road. Flowering trees and shrubs overhanging the old road create an ideal habitat for songbirds, and the smooth walking surface allows you to look around to see them as you go. We spotted a scarlet tanager, warblers, and vireos.

At the yellow gate, turn right and walk on the boat access road, following the blue blazes. At 5.3 miles, you reach a large trail sign. (The Frank Gantz Trail turns right for 3.3 miles from Gouldsboro to Tobyhanna State Park.)

The Prospect Rock Trail turns left on an old camp road and crosses several access roads to the lake. At 5.7 miles, you reach the parking lot and your car.

17. BRADY'S LAKE

Distance	4.9 miles
Elevation	140 feet
Time to hike	2 hours
Surface	Rocky woods road, railroad grade
Interesting features	Quiet, peaceful lake (electric motors only); old railroad grade
Facilities	Jiffy John at the parking lot; no water or picnic facilities
Hunting	Yes

Directions

From I-80 (Exit 43) east of White Haven:

1. North on PA 115 for 1.3 miles to PA 940
2. Turn right (east) on PA 940 for 4.8 miles to Fish Commission Road
3. Turn left at Fish Commission Road for 3.3 miles to the parking lot

Coordinates 41°09'47"N; 75°31'41"W

Brady's Lake was built for the ice industry in the early 1890s. Ice harvesting continued and was profitable into the 1930s, until the use of electricity and refrigeration became widespread. The area was later acquired by the federal government and became part of the Tobyhanna Military Reservation. The Fish and Game Commission acquired Brady's Lake in 1949; the lake is located within State Game Lands 127.

Begin walking at the south end of the lake; proceed west around a metal gate. The asphalt path crosses an overflow outlet on a wooden bridge. A U.S. Geological Survey marker on the bridge identifies the elevation as 1,717 feet. Then cross a 40-foot wooden bridge over the main spillway, Trout Creek. The asphalt path proceeds over the earthen dam.

The trail continues as a woods road along the western edge of the lake through a red pine and spruce plantation. At .6 mile, reach an intersection with another woods road, your return route. Turn right (north) along the lake. At .7 mile, you pass the stone foundation remains of a large icehouse. The ice was cut from the lake by workers with special saws and loaded onto sleds. Horses dragged

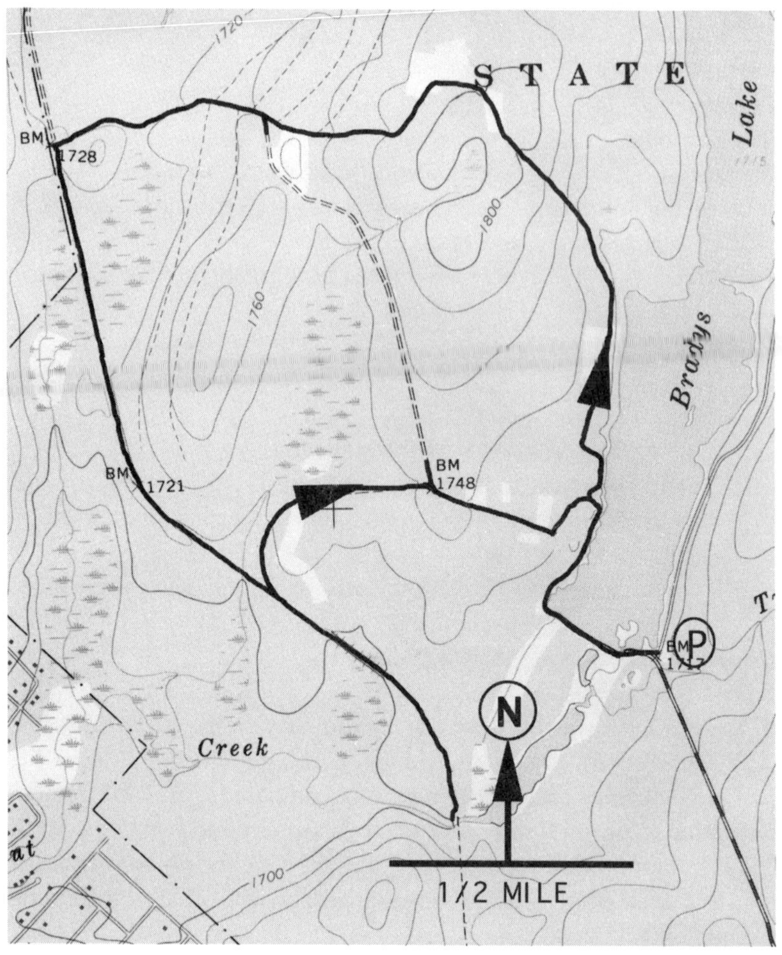

the sleds to insulated buildings, where the ice was stored. Forty thousand tons of ice may have been stored here. During the summer, the ice was loaded onto railcars at the nearby spur and shipped to customers in Wilkes-Barre and throughout the region.

At 1 mile, turn away from the lake and through a grassy meadow, still on a woods road. The trail leads through mixed young hardwoods (birch, beech, black cherry) and then occasional open fields and feedlots. In the middle of one field is a large old apple tree.

Just after reentering the woods after a meadow, an old woods road comes in from the left. Continue straight ahead—west. There are some very old mixed evergreen trees along the trail—hemlock, spruce, and an old white pine almost 6 feet in diameter.

At 2.5 miles, reach an abandoned railroad grade of the old Wilkes-Barre and Eastern Railroad line. An orange gate is straight ahead. Turn left (south) on the railroad grade. The trail is easy walking and lined with blueberries along both sides for the next mile, as you pass through mixed hardwoods and then swamp. At times the grade is elevated 15 feet, and at times it runs through a cut below the forest floor.

In June, snapping turtles climb out of the swamp and lay eggs in holes dug in the loose gravel ballast of the track bed. Most of these nests (up to 100 percent in some years) are dug up within a few days by predators, especially skunks and raccoons. Piles of broken shells beside shallow holes indicate disturbed nests. Judging from the number of them, there must be a lot of turtles (and their predators) in the swamp. We almost stepped on a particularly aggressive snapper about a foot across. She definitely resented our efforts to get a good picture. If you see a snapper, keep your distance—they can deliver a nasty bite.

Pass a U.S. Geological Survey marker (elevation 1,721 feet—only 4 feet higher than the lake) on the right. Next, watch carefully for a small stream that runs under the elevated track bed. Just after the stream, at 3.5 miles, turn left on a grassy woods road, a spur of the former railroad grade.

If you continue on the railroad grade, you will reach Trout Creek, which drains Brady's Lake, but the bridge is out. The stream can be crossed only after a dry spell. If you decide to do so, a left turn on the Locust Lake Trail—1,000 feet beyond the stream—will take you back to the lake access road and return you to your car, for a total distance of 6.1 miles.

For this hike, though, turn left on the grassy road at 3.5 miles, immediately bearing left again. (The road to the right goes to a feedlot.) The game commission has cut trees and brush in a 20-foot swath on each side of the road. The brush provides cover and food for game animals and birds. Pass several feedlots; the road jogs right at a road intersection, then continues east toward the lake.

At the lake, turn right on the woods road you hiked in on, and retrace your steps to your car.

18. BIG PINE HILL

Distance	5.1 miles
Elevation	370 feet
Time to hike	2½ hours
Surface	Rocky trail, grassy woods road
Interesting features	Views
Facilities	None
Hunting	Yes

Directions

From I-80 (Exit 43) east of White Haven:

1. North on PA 115 for 5.8 miles to River Road
2. Turn right on River Road (SR 2040) for 4.9 miles to Bear Lake Road
3. Turn left on Bear Lake Road (SR 2016) for 4.2 miles to the trailhead on the right

Coordinates 41°13'08"N; 75°37'54"W

Begin this hike on the Pinchot Trail in the Lackawanna State Forest at the large trail sign. Frank Gantz, a retired truck driver, scouted the terrain and laid out the trail, which was constructed in 1975 by the Youth Conservation Corps and the Sierra Club of Northeast Pennsylvania. The trail was dedicated in 1982 and named for Gifford Pinchot, twice governor of Pennsylvania and the first chief of the U.S. Forest Service. The Powder Magazine Trail leads uphill a short distance to a well-made box containing a trail register and maps of the system. Mr. Gantz still looks after his trail; we met him in June 1998 delivering a supply of maps here.

The main trail in the 23-mile Pinchot System is blazed blue. Side trails are red- or orange-blazed. At .5 mile, you leave the blue-blazed main trail and turn left on the orange-blazed Pine Hill Trail. To your left are ferns, to your right is a stand of pine and spruce trees, an abandoned plantation. On our last visit, crows loudly squawking and flying among the trees appeared to be involved in a territorial dispute.

Turn left on the Frank Gantz Trail at .8 mile. The starts of trails throughout the system are well marked with signs. The trail is rocky, with expanses of sheep laurel and blueberries. You cross several

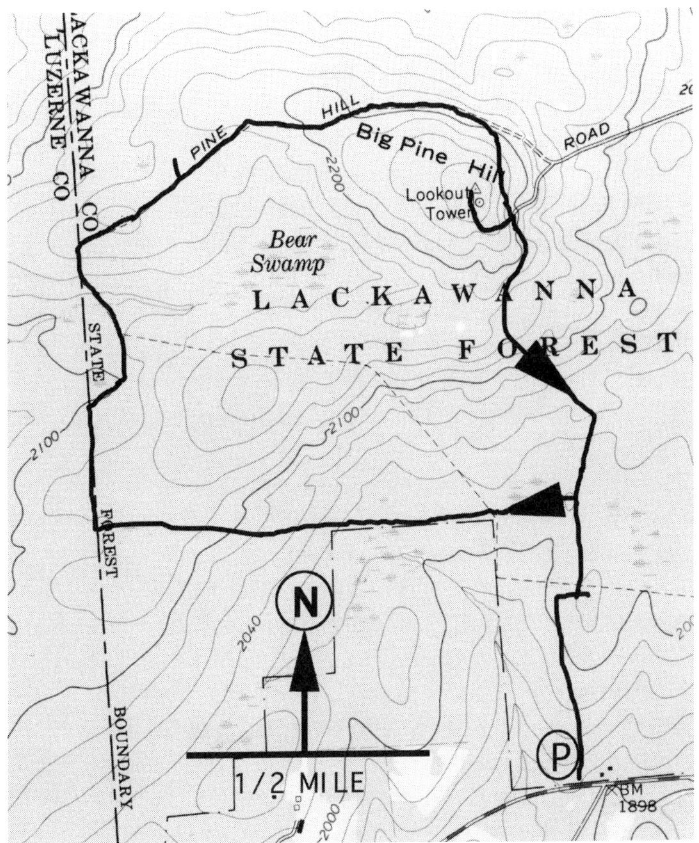

grassy snowmobile trail cuts in the woods—just pick up the orange blazes on the other side.

Turn right (north) at an intersection with the blue-blazed White Line Trail at 1.8 miles. Private property is to your left at the border between Lackawanna and Luzerne Counties. The trail is fairly straight and was probably a boundary road. The trail skirts a swampy area, then returns to the boundary. At 2.3 miles, the trail turns right, away from the boundary, for easy walking on an old grassy road. You are able to see some distance ahead along the road and are likely to observe deer, grouse, or turkeys at the woods edge.

The main trail turns left on the Scrub Oak Trail; continue straight ahead, following red or orange blazes on the grassy Pine Hill Trail. Bear Swamp is to your right, but the trail remains dry. At

3.3 miles, the road ends at a yellow gate. Turn right into the woods. Soon the trail circles a massive rock outcropping perhaps 20 feet high on your right. Big Pine Hill is capped by this table of resistant sandstone, while much of the surrounding terrain has eroded away.

Turn right at a dirt road for a .2-mile side trip to the top of Big Pine Hill. From a flat rock table at 2,200 feet, you have a 360-degree view of the surrounding Pocono Plateau. Climb a 25-foot observation tower for an even better view. The vegetation here is stunted because of the poor soil and constant wind and consists mostly of blueberries, scrub oaks, and pines only 15 feet high. To the southeast, you can see Brady's Lake (see Hike No. 17). Looking north, seven low mountain ridges are visible on a clear day, some topped with microwave towers.

Return down the dirt road and turn right, continuing on the Pine Hill Trail. You lose elevation quickly on the rocky, eroded trail. Footing is a bit difficult over a boulder field.

Complete the loop where the Frank Gantz Trail comes in from the right. Continue straight ahead. From here, you retrace your steps to the Powder Magazine Trail. Turn right slightly uphill, then go back down past the trail register to reach your car.

There are many other possible routes through the system. For an excellent free map of the entire Pinchot Trail, write to the Forest District Manager, Forest District 11, Room 401, State Office Building, 100 Lackawanna Avenue, Scranton, PA 18503-1923.

19. CHOKE CREEK TRAIL

Distance	6 miles
Elevation	390 feet
Time to hike	3 hours
Surface	Rocky woods trail, grassy woods road
Interesting features	Choke Creek, beaver community
Facilities	None
Hunting	Yes

Directions

From I-80 (Exit 43) east of White Haven:

1. North on PA 115 for 5.8 miles to River Road
2. Turn right on River Road (SR 2040) for 4.9 miles to Bear Lake Road
3. Turn left on Bear Lake Road (SR 2016) for 1.8 miles to Tannery Road
4. Turn left on Tannery Road for 1.8 miles to the trailhead on the left

Coordinates 41°11'58"N; 75°37'54"W

This hike in the Pinchot Trail System takes you along a very scenic stream, Choke Creek. At the parking lot, there is a large trail sign indicating the Choke Creek Trail as 5.5 miles long, which underestimates the distance. This hike begins on the red-blazed Choke Creek side trail. The main trail in the 23-mile Pinchot system is blue-blazed.

Begin walking back southeast on Tannery Road for .6 mile, following red blazes. Mountain laurel blooms in June. Double red blazes at a metal gate signal a turn to the right on a grassy woods road that is closed to traffic. The first half mile is part of the Howley Orienteering Area, used as a compass course. A dense pine and hemlock forest is on your left.

At 1.4 miles, watch carefully again for double red blazes, where you turn right into the woods on a rocky path. After passing some large red oaks, you cross Butler Run on stepping-stones. In spring, look for painted trillium, a delicate woodland flower in shades of white or pale pink. Trillium likes moist woodland environments and can be identified by its characteristic three leaves and three petals.

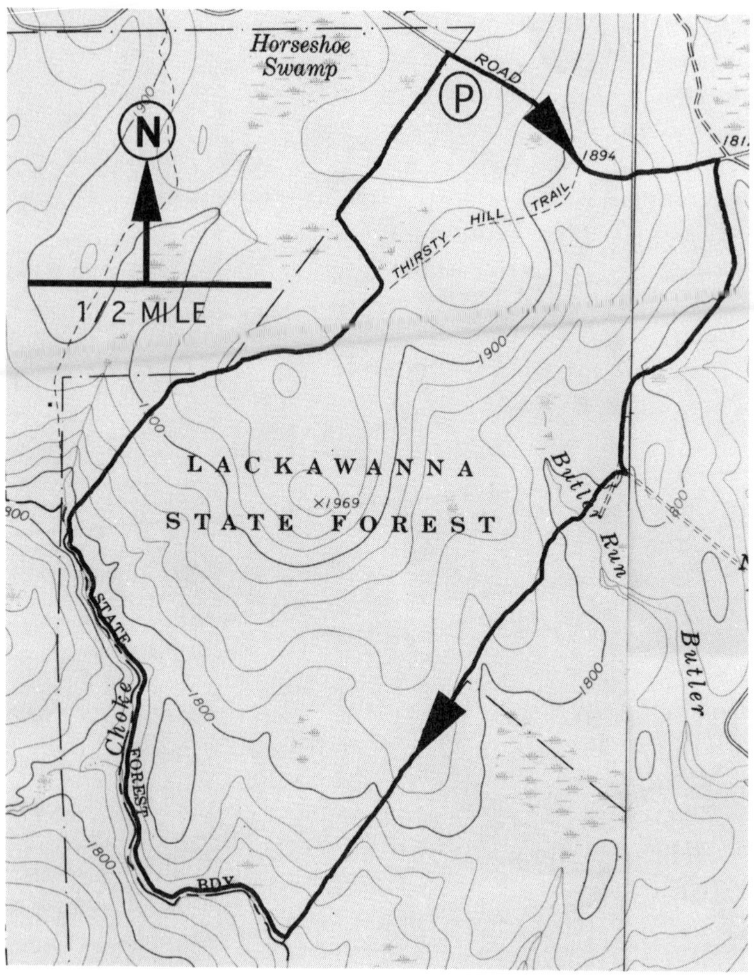

The woods here are fairly open, with alternating acres of ferns, blueberries and sheep laurel, white and gray birches. At 2 miles, you reach an intersection with the blue-blazed Butler Run Trail; turn right (west). Immediately cross a small tributary. Private property signs for a sportsmen's club lie on the park boundary to your left.

Reach Choke Creek and turn right upstream. The trail turns away from the creek and then back toward it several times. In wet areas, sphagnum moss cushions your step as you cross open water from hummock to hummock. A beaver community has dammed the creek at a bend. You are unlikely to spot beavers, as they are primarily nocturnal. However, you have a good view of the dam, the beaver lodge, and the drowned trees standing in the pond. The trail has been partially flooded too, and you'll be glad you wore your boots.

The trail turns right (south) through a stand of balsam fir and tamarack, then skirts another boggy area at 4.2 miles. It leads gradually uphill but continues rocky and poorly drained. The trail turns right 90 degrees; then rhododendrons crowd in on both sides, up to 15 feet high, creating a tunnel effect. Highbush blueberries, a favorite with bears, ripen in July. Tannery Road and the parking lot are just ahead.

PART TWO

RIDGE AND VALLEY PROVINCE

Carbon, Schuylkill, and Berks Counties

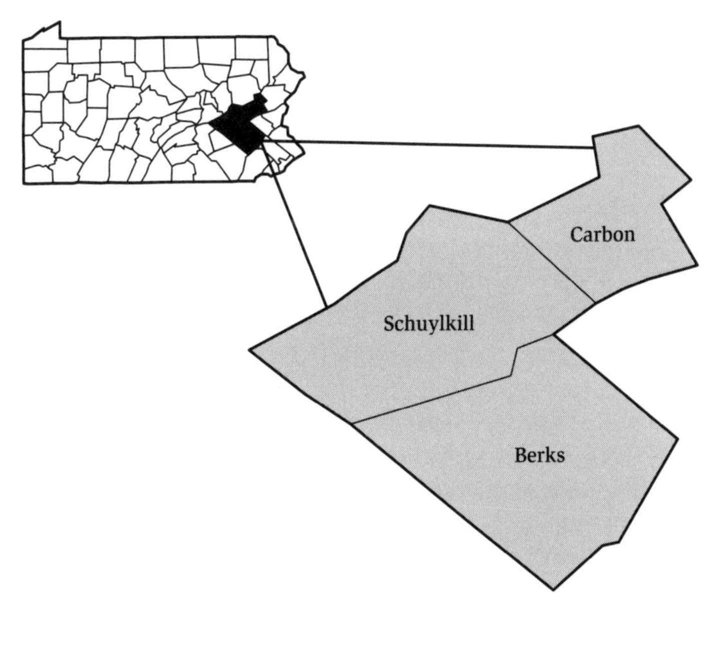

20. MARGY'S TRAIL

Distance	3.8 miles
Elevation	500 feet
Time to hike	2¾ hours
Surface	Extremely rocky woods trail, game-lands boundary line, power-line road
Interesting features	Boulder fields, view from Lake Mountain
Facilities	None
Hunting	Yes

Directions

From I-80 (Exit 43) south of Wilkes-Barre:

1. South on PA 115 for 1.9 miles to PA 903
2. Turn right (south) on PA 903 for 2.6 miles to the parking lot on the left

Coordinates 41°02'10"N; 75°35'02"W

Although not very long, this hike in State Game Lands 129 is demanding. Be sure to wear sturdy hiking boots, as a misstep in a rocky crevice can easily turn an ankle. The trail is orange-blazed; it is unusual to find a maintained trail in game lands. The game-lands boundary line is not a trail and is fairly rough going.

Begin by crossing PA 903 to the trail as it enters the forest. After a few feet, the orange-blazed trail splits. Bear right on a rocky, moss-covered trail. (The trail to your left will be your return route.) The gorge steepens on both sides, filled with rhododendrons and hemlocks. You can hear an underground stream that surfaces here and there as springs, seepage from Big Boulder Lake ahead.

Follow the orange blazes until the game-lands boundary at .5 mile, marked with white paint on every third or fourth tree. Turn left and climb out of the gorge on a steep, rocky hillside. Rhododendrons and hemlocks give way to hardwoods, mountain and sheep laurel, and blueberries. We found plenty of bear sign on the trail throughout this hike.

The property beyond the boundary belongs to the Big Boulder Ski Resort. The trail continues gradually uphill, through several boulder fields. The rocks are mostly of pink and gray sandstone. Many contain inclusions of granite pebbles, exposed by the weathering of the surrounding softer sandstone. Between the piled and

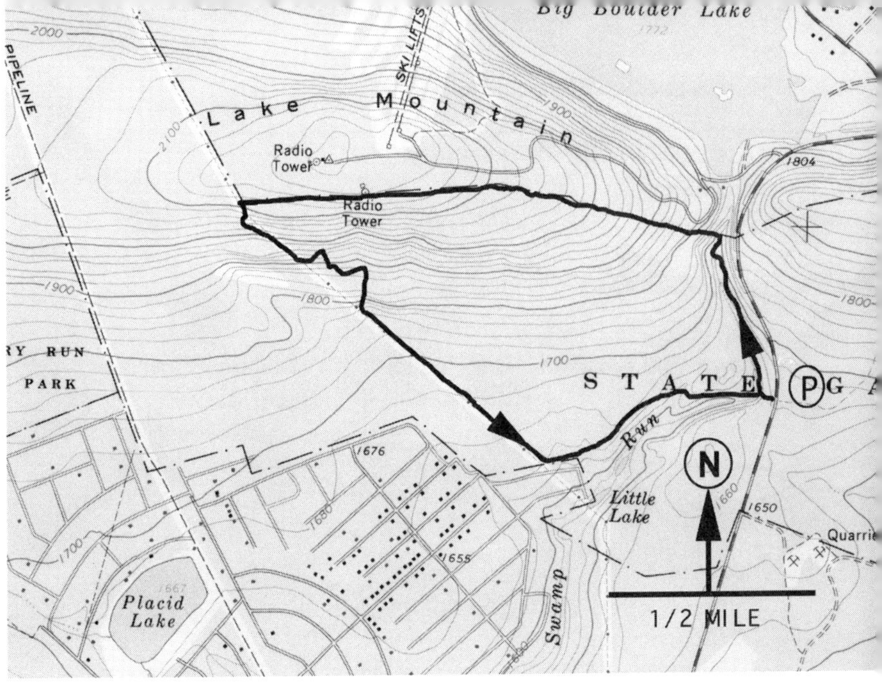

tumbled boulders are many smaller rocks, well hidden in thick blueberries and laurel. There seem to be tiny gnomes hidden as well, who are expert at untying bootlaces every few feet.

At 1.3 miles, you reach two microwave towers. Trees become more stunted, mostly chestnut oak, bear oak, red pine, and mountain ash, whose bright red-orange berries in fall stand out against the light-colored rocks. The trail continues along the rocky Lake Mountain ridge to a power transmission line at 1.8 miles.

From here you have a fine view south to Placid Lake and beyond to Stony Ridge and Pohopoco Mountain. Turn left to follow the power-line road as it descends steeply around a rocky hillside, then continues downhill. The road ends at another jumbled rock pile. Turn left to enter the woods on the orange-blazed trail. The trail winds through mixed hardwoods and rhododendrons, and rejoins the power-line road. Turn left, continuing downhill. Watch carefully for the white game-lands boundary at 3 miles, just before the road starts to go uphill. Turn left to reenter the woods. To your right, just on the other side of the boundary, is a shooting range.

Pick up orange blazes as you continue through hardwoods, then hemlocks and rhododendrons. Cross an intermittent stream, Swamp Run. Soon you hear the traffic on PA 903; complete the loop, and return to your car.

21. BELTZVILLE STATE PARK

Distance	4.5 miles
Elevation	255 feet
Time to hike	2¼ hours
Surface	Rocky trail, mown grassy roads, trails recently blazed
Interesting features	Lovely views of Wild Creek Cove from high on a hemlock- and laurel-covered ridge, Wild Creek Falls
Facilities	None
Hunting	Yes

Directions

From northeast extension of PA Turnpike (I-476; Exit 34) south of Wilkes-Barre:

1. South on PA 209 for .1 mile to Harrity Road
2. Turn left at Harrity Road for .1 mile to Pohopoco Drive
3. Turn right on Pohopoco Drive (TR 435) for 6.4 miles to grassy pull-off on the right, by a sign "Christman Trail"

Coordinates 40°53'20"N; 75°34'14"W

The U.S. Corps of Engineers built Beltzville Lake in the late 1960s and early 1970s. The lake was officially opened for recreation in May 1972. Some of the trails have been relocated in the past few years but are clearly blazed.

From the pull-off, walk south past a yellow-and-black metal fence on a mown grassy trail. A sign warns of the tick hazard in this area. In grassy areas everywhere in northeastern Pennsylvania, it is a good idea to wear a long-sleeved shirt and pants, and to tuck your pants legs into your socks. After your hike, inspect your clothes and skin for the tiny pests.

Old farm fields and orchards lie along both sides of the well-marked trail. Notice a line of black walnut trees on the right, and bluebird nesting boxes in the meadow. At .3 mile, another trail comes in from the left (your return route).

Turn right on a green-blazed trail to enter a dense hemlock forest leading to a small stream at the bottom of a ravine. Follow the stream, then climb up to rejoin the yellow-blazed Christman Trail.

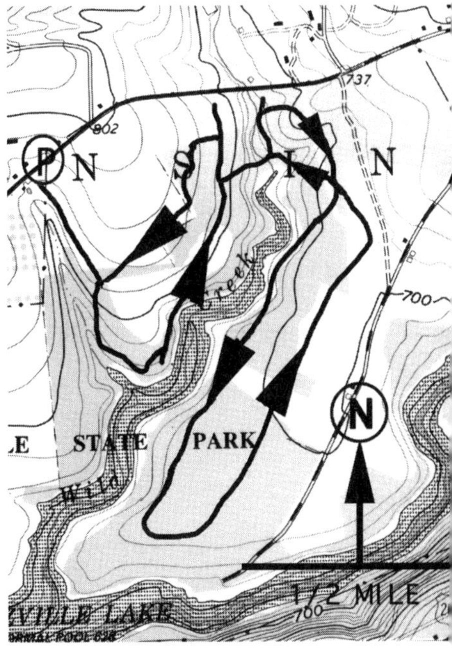

At 1 mile, you reach a T intersection; turn left (north), following the yellow blazes. Continue walking through old orchards and meadow on a woods road. At 1.3 miles, turn right on the blue-and-white-blazed Falls Trail. Go downhill on a shale-covered trail toward Wild Creek, through a stand of dense hemlocks and mountain laurel, in bloom in June. Cross Wild Creek, 30 feet wide, on a sturdy wooden footbridge at 1.4 miles.

Walk along the creek upstream to Wild Creek Falls, tumbling 30 feet over large boulders. The trail has been relocated in this area; watch carefully for the double blue blazes indicating a turn to the right. Climb out of the gorge through hemlocks and mixed hardwoods. At 1.8 miles, you reach a 70-foot-wide mown clearing (a water right-of-way). Watch for the white blazes for the Cove Ridge Trail. Cross a small stream on a wooden bridge, then walk up the field to reenter the hemlock forest. The trail leads steeply uphill on a hemlock- and rhododendron-covered hillside.

At 2 miles, reach the top of the ridge. The ground slopes steeply away to the right, dropping to Wild Creek several hundred feet below. Walk along the edge of the ridge, with views to the ravine and creek far below. Soon the creek widens to Wild Creek Cove. The trail is fairly easy walking on hemlock needles through the dark forest. As the cove widens to the lake, the trail turns east, then north away from the ridge through competing small mixed hardwoods, hemlocks, and ferns. The undergrowth is quite thick here; the trail is almost a tunnel through vegetation—an abrupt change from the openness beneath the mature hemlocks along the ridgeline.

You reach the mown field again at 3.1 miles. Cross the small bridge and turn left on the blue-and-white-blazed trail through thick rhododendron along a small seasonal stream. Return to the larger bridge over Wild Creek at 3.9 miles. Cross the bridge and head uphill, turning right on the Christman Trail. The trail is blazed white, blue, and yellow.

Follow the yellow blazes, turning left on the Christman Trail, through mixed hardwoods. Watch carefully for the yellow blazes indicating another left turn just before the Wild Creek Trailhead parking lot. Follow the grassy road. The woods are to the left, and an open meadow is to the right, filled with wildflowers in spring and summer. Turn right at 4.3 miles to retrace your steps and return to your car.

22. HICKORY RUN STATE PARK

Distance	13.1 miles
Elevation	1,230 feet
Time to hike	6½ hours
Surface	Rocky woods trails, old roads
Interesting features	Boulder field, Hawk Falls
Facilities	None
Hunting	Yes

Directions

From I-80 (Exit 41) at White Haven south of Wilkes-Barre:

1. East on PA 534 for 9.8 miles (Hickory Run Park office is at 5.1 miles, where park maps are available)
2. Park at the parking lot on the right for "Organized Tenting Area"

Coordinates 41°00'50"N; 75°37'44"W

This long hike through Hickory Run State Park is a double loop and takes you to the two major attractions of this large park. First you visit Hawk Falls, a lovely waterfall in a hemlock and rhododendron ravine, and then remarkable Boulder Field, a reminder of the last ice age 20,000 years ago and the best example of a boulder field in the eastern United States.

Begin walking on the dirt road past tent campsites. Continue around a yellow-and-black metal gate and follow a rocky road down through rhododendrons over 15 feet high to Mud Run. Mud Run, contrary to its name, is a clear, free-running, artificial-lures-only stream and was popular with fishermen angling for trout the day we were there. The trail has infrequent red blazes and is often muddy, but it was recently cleared and is easy to follow. Follow the stream a short distance and then climb up very steeply to a ridgeline at 1.8 miles to avoid steep terrain and dense vegetation along Mud Run. The trail descends to stream level again at 2 miles at a tree with double yellow blazes. Turn left and follow Mud Run down a short distance, where it is joined by Hawk Run at Hawk Run Falls. Retrace your steps to the tree with double yellow blazes. Follow the Hawk Falls Trail on a rocky woods road out of the gorge. A short side

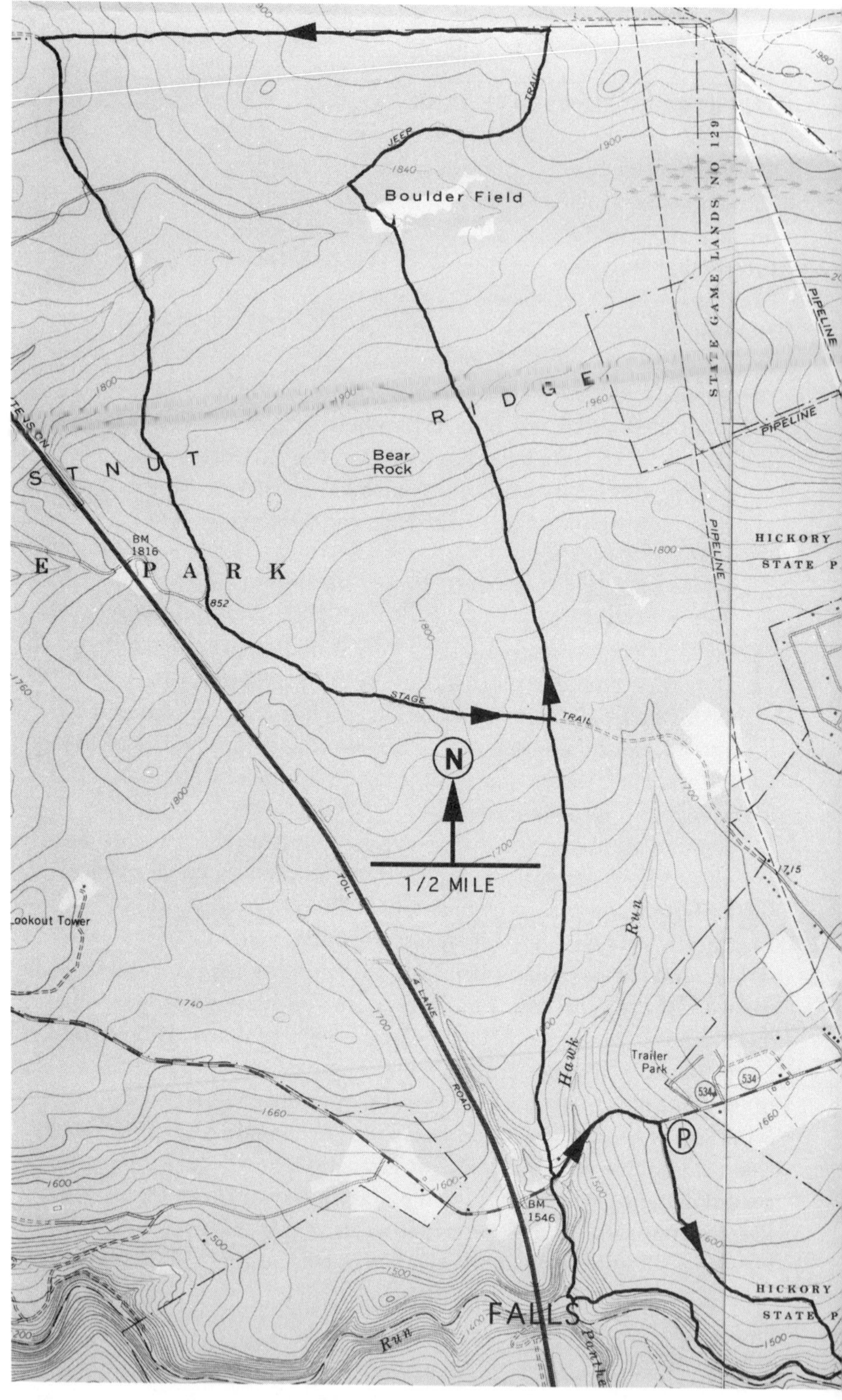

Boulder Field
JEEP
TRAIL
STATE GAME LANDS NO 129
PIPELINE
R I D G E
STNUT
Bear
Rock
E P A R K
BM
1816
852
STAGE
TRAIL
HICKORY
STATE P
N
1/2 MILE
TOLL
4 LANE
ROAD
Lookout Tower
Run
Hawk
Trailer
Park
534
P
BM
1546
FALLS
Run
Panthe
HICKORY
STATE P

trail on the left takes you to a rock outcropping at the top of the falls. Cross Hawk Run on stepping-stones (take along extra socks—you may get your feet wet), and reach PA 534 at 2.5 miles.

Cross PA 534 and pick up a trail at the east end of the parking lot. Wooden steps climb up to an old apple orchard. Cross the orchard and reenter the woods at the yellow-blazed Boulder Field Trail, a rocky woods road. The intersection with the Stage Trail, and the start of the loop to Boulder Field, is the halfway point.

The woods road narrows to a rocky trail. Rhododendrons are in bloom from mid-June to mid-July. In a stand of hemlocks, we surprised, and were surprised by, a medium-sized black bear 100 feet ahead of us. He was busy turning over rocks in the middle of the trail apparently searching for grubs. He saw us at the same time we saw him, turned tail, and ran away from us up the trail.

Quite suddenly the woods end, and you are at the edge of Boulder Field, a barren expanse of rocks 400 feet wide and more than a quarter mile long. The rocks are at least 12 feet deep and are composed of red sandstone at the north end and red conglomerates with white quartz pebbles at the south end. There are a few lichens on some of the boulders but no soil to support other plant life. An old-growth forest of black spruce and white pine surrounds and has begun to invade the edges of the boulder field.

Cautiously cross the boulders to the parking lot on the other side. Boulder Field is the headwaters of Hickory Run, and if you listen closely, you can hear water rushing under the boulders. Walk to the end of the parking lot and pick up the Stone Trail. The trail goes to the boundary line and intersects with a power line and pipeline at 6.3 miles. This intersection is the approximate stopping point of the glacier's southernmost extent (or terminal moraine, in geologists' terms). Turn left. The trail is level, easy walking on crushed shale through huckleberries, sheep laurel, and ferns. Private Property signs are posted on the right.

At a hemlock forest at 7.8 miles, turn left (south) on Fourth Run Trail, a rocky woods road closed to traffic. At 8.2 miles, cross the park road to the boulder field, continuing south on a park road open to one-way traffic. Cross Hickory Run on a culvert at 8.6 miles. At 9.7 miles, the road bends to the right; continue straight ahead on an old woods road, and in 50 yards, turn left on the Stage Trail. This woods road, now closed to vehicles, was once the major stage route between Bethlehem and Wilkes-Barre. At 11.2 miles, complete the Boulder Field Loop and turn right to retrace your steps to PA 534 at 12.7 miles. Turn left on PA 534, walking on the left side to face traffic, to return to your car at 13.1 miles.

Additional boulder fields are found at Hawk Mountain Sanctuary (Hike No. 25), Margy's Trail (Hike No. 20), and Wolf Swamp and Deep Lake (Hike No. 14).

23. SWITCHBACK RAILROAD

Distance	10.5 miles
Elevation	660 feet
Time to hike	5 hours
Surface	Abandoned railroad grade, rocky woods road
Interesting features	Historic gravity railroad grade, scenic views
Facilities	Rest rooms, water, picnic facilities at the main park office
Hunting	Yes

Directions

From northeast extension of PA Turnpike (I-476; Exit 34) south of Wilkes-Barre:

1. South on PA 209 for 5.8 miles to Broadway
2. Turn left on Broadway (SR 3012) for 3.4 miles to parking lot on the left

Coordinates 40°50'49"W; 75°47'55"N

Anthracite coal was discovered in Summit Hill in 1791, and the Lehigh Valley Coal and Navigation Company was established to bring it to market. A primitive rail system, invented in 1827, brought the coal from the mines by gravity to the Lehigh River in Mauch Chunk—now Jim Thorpe—Pennsylvania. Coal was loaded onto wooden cars and run downhill, their speed controlled by hand brakes. Mules hauled the empty cars up the mountain on the same rails. The mules traveled back to Mauch Chunk in special stable cars attached to the coal cars and were fed en route—the first railroad dining cars.

In 1844, the invention of the steam-powered engine eliminated the need for mules to return the cars to the summit. Stationary steam engines at the top of inclined planes hauled the empty cars up the mountain. The Mount Pisgah plane in Jim Thorpe hoisted the cars 740 feet up; the cars then moved across the south side of the mountain by gravity on tracks (the "light track") to Summit Hill. The Mount Jefferson plane in Summit Hill lifted the cars an additional 470 feet. The cars were loaded and rolled down the "loaded track" to Jim Thorpe. The light track crossed over the loaded track at Five Mile

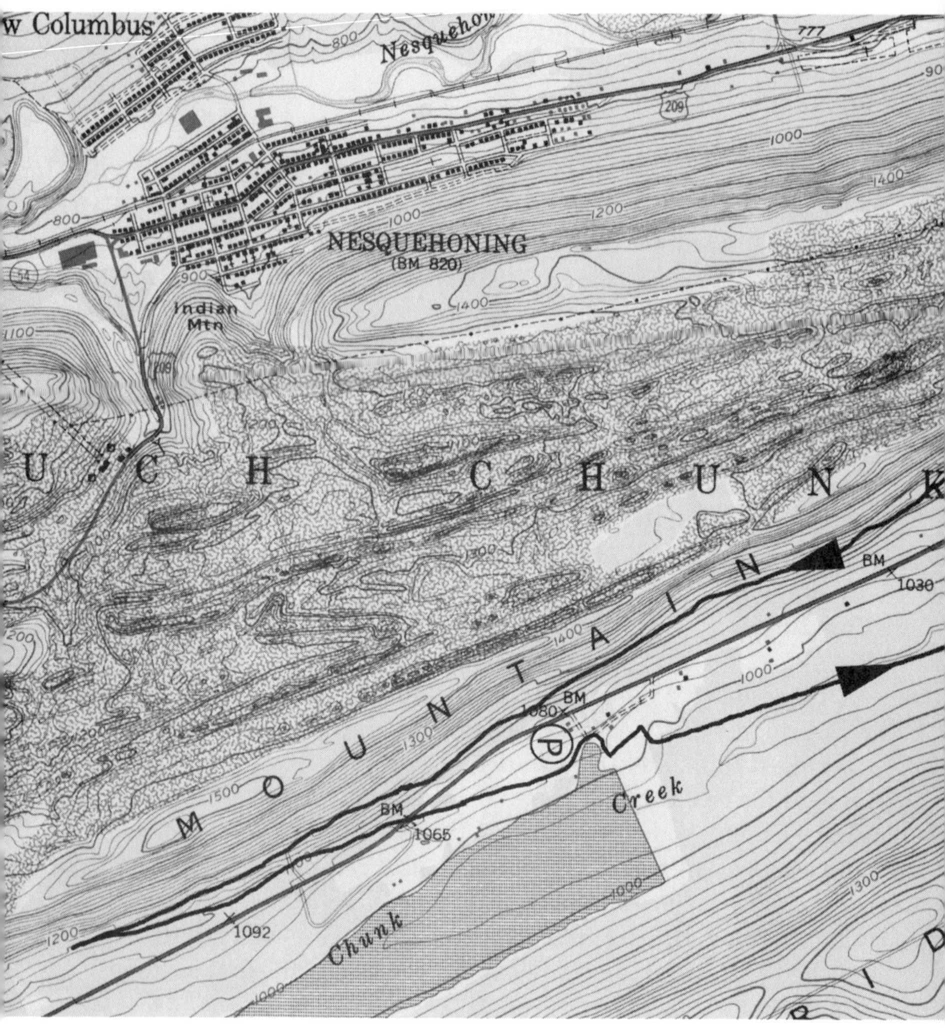

Tree Bridge. The two tracks and crossover at Five Mile Tree form a rough figure-eight pattern. An additional loop track was built for passenger cars, and additional spur tracks were built between the planes to service various mines between the planes. A side track ran off the line in Summit Hill and switchbacked down the north side of the mountain; this branch gave the railroad its name, "Switchback Railroad." This early railroad inspired present-day amusement park roller-coaster rides.

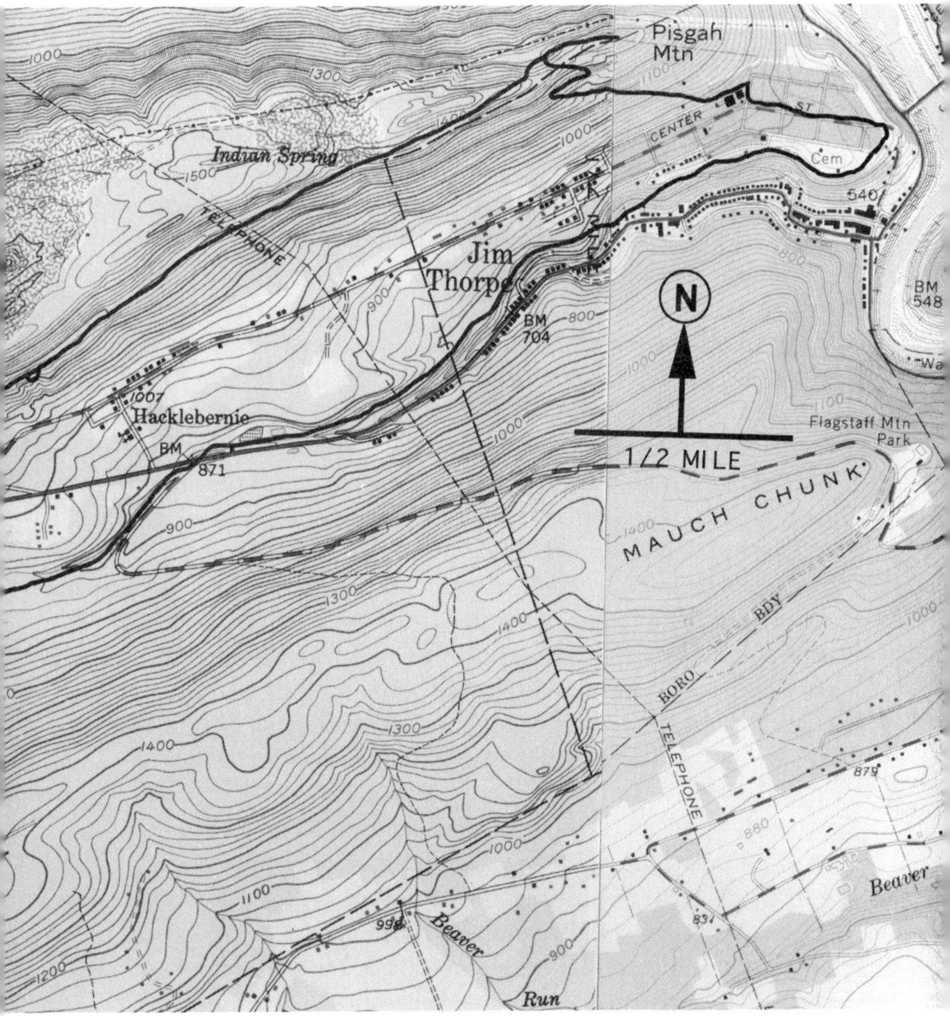

The cars were unloaded in Mauch Chunk to barges, which transported the coal down the Lehigh River on an ingenious system of canals and locks and on to Easton, Philadelphia, Baltimore, and Wilmington. The gravity railroad became obsolete in 1872 with the invention of the mobile steam locomotive. Major railroads then began servicing the mines directly. However, the Switchback Railroad took on a second life as a tourist attraction, providing turn-of-the-century thrill seekers with wild rides. The Great Depression and economic decline led to the Switchback Railroad's ceasing operations in 1933.

The gravity railroad and canal system was at the cutting edge of engineering technology. This achievement in the early nineteenth century was key to the rapid industrialization of the Northeast. It must have been just as marvelous to people then as the computer and communication revolution is to us today.

Begin walking toward Mauch Chunk Lake, around a spillway for the dam. After an intersection of dirt roads, turn left at a bench to pick up the easy-to-follow grade of the down, or loaded, track. The trail parallels Mauch Chunk Creek on your left through thick hemlocks and mountain laurel. At 1.6 miles, the grade curves left at a small dam for the Jim Thorpe water supply. At 1.8 miles, you reach the road to Flagstaff Park. This intersection once served as a transfer point for trolleys to carry visitors to the pool and picnic facilities at Flagstaff Park.

Cross the main road from town on a diagonal. Pass an orange bridge with a No Trespassing sign, then cross Mauch Chunk Creek on a culvert. A water tank, buildings, and water treatment facility on your left are surrounded by No Trespassing signs. The tumbling creek to your right contains the concrete remains of the old railroad bridge. Walk east on the dirt road to the railroad grade as it reenters dense woods.

At 3 miles, you cross a paved road that leads from the town of Jim Thorpe on the right steeply uphill to Upper Jim Thorpe on the left. Notice the rail embedded in the pavement. The grade is cut into the narrow hillside between these communities. Shortly, you cross another paved road that leads from the opera house; then you walk through a grassy area and reenter the woods.

Drainage in this area appears to be affected by development in Upper Jim Thorpe, as the track bed becomes quite wet and muddy. A second grade on your left parallels for a short distance. Pass the ruins of a stone mansion on your right. On your left, a large church is followed by a cemetery behind a high retaining wall.

At 3.9 miles, you reach the road leading from the Asa Packer Mansion, the courthouse, and CNJ Railroad Station. Turn left, leaving the railroad grade, onto Center Avenue for three blocks to the junior high school. Turn right on Pine Avenue, then left on North Avenue. Pass a couple of garages in disrepair on your left, then turn right on an extremely steep and rocky wagon road. The old road, impassable by most vehicles, switchbacks up to the summit of Mount Pisgah at 5.2 miles.

You first encounter the concrete remains of a reservoir that supplied water to the engine house boilers. Turn right to the ruins of the engine house itself. Notice the remains of the metal smokestack and rails, which were recycled to reinforce the concrete foundation. From here you can look down the Mount Pisgah inclined plane on the east side of the mountain, where empty cars were hauled up the mountain. This is the start of the light track.

There is a sag in elevation between the engine house and the mountain ridge, that was bridged by a trestle. Walk west past the piers that supported the trestle to the ridge, with fine views to the Lehigh River, Jim Thorpe, and the mountains to the north, east, and south.

The grade continues west, gradually descending from the ridgeline. At 5.9 miles, water from Indian Spring at the summit flows down the mountainside. Water piped from here filled the reservoir for the engine boilers. The grade leads gently downhill through second-growth hardwoods and laurel.

At 6.8 miles, the track bed falls steeply away beside a rock face. A cut below the rock projects into the hillside at the Hacklebernie Mine entrance. Mine tailings extend out from the entrance. The managers of the Summit Hill Mine continually searched for coal seams closer to the Lehigh River. However, the Hacklebernie deposit was inferior in both quantity and quality and proved unprofitable. The 30-foot gap over the mine entrance can be carefully crossed on a 3- to 5-inch ledge when dry and by the surefooted; otherwise, the safer course is to walk down and around the collapse to pick up the grade on the other side.

At 9.5 miles, you reach the crossover at Five Mile Tree, named for a tree that marked the 5-mile point from the base of the Mount Pisgah plane. Note the remains of the bridge, where the light track crossed over the loaded track. A short connector track linked the two tracks, allowing coal loaded from Hacklebernie and other mines along the light track to return to Mauch Chunk without having to travel to Summit Hill. Turn left on the down, or loaded, track. A lot of coal was spilled from the loaded cars here (the Visitors Center at the Mauch Chunk Switchback Depot sells small chunks of coal for 75 cents). The down track passes a trail register between two houses at 10 miles. Cross the highway between Jim Thorpe and Summit Hill on a diagonal at 10.3 miles. Walk past the park entrance and Switchback replica car on a siding. At 10.5 miles, you reach the lake and your car.

The Switchback Gravity Railroad Foundation holds easements over much of the route. There are lots of additional trails in the area, including a 5-mile footpath around Mauch Chunk Lake. You can pick up a map at the park office or contact Carbon County Parks and Recreation Department, 625 Lentz Trail, Jim Thorpe, PA 18229. Or visit the Gravity Railroad Foundation website at www.jtasd.k12.pa.us/switchback.

24. GLEN ONOKO RUN

Distance	2.1 miles
Elevation	900 feet
Time to hike	2 hours
Surface	Rough, steep, rocky gorge trail
Interesting features	Hemlock gorge, three major waterfalls, views
Facilities	None
Hunting	Yes

Directions

From northeast extension of PA Turnpike (I-476; Exit 34) south of Wilkes-Barre:

1. South on PA 209 for 7.8 miles to PA 903
2. Turn right (north) on PA 903, cross the Lehigh River, and continue three blocks (.2 mile)
3. Continue straight on Front Street for .3 mile to Glen Onoko Access Area; turn left
4. Turn left on access road 1.6 miles to parking lot

Coordinates 40°53'04"N; 75°45'32"W

This short but very steep trail is for surefooted and strong-legged hikers with some experience. Although just over 2 miles in length, the trail is steep, rocky, and often eroded. It is unsafe after rain or during the winter because of slippery conditions. You will be using hand-over-foot rock climbing in some areas, very close to steep drops of a hundred feet or more. However, for waterfall and climbing enthusiasts, this hike is worth it. Seven distinct waterfalls, including three major ones over 30 feet high, tumble 900 feet in 1 mile through the narrow, hemlock-filled gorge.

Although the access road and parking lot are in Lehigh Gorge State Park, this hike is entirely within State Game Lands 141. From the parking lot, descend steep wooden steps on a trail that turns around and passes underneath the access road and two active rail lines. (Do not cross the tracks at the parking lot—to do so is dangerous as well as against the law.)

The Lehigh River is to your left. The floodplain of the river is narrow because of the steep terrain. Shrubs cannot withstand the

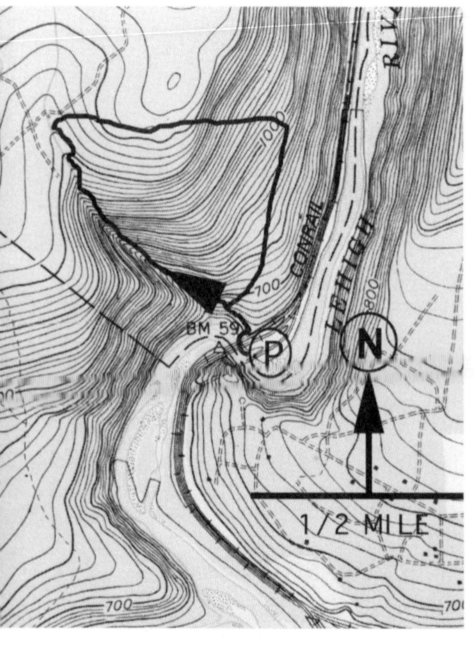

frequent flooding, but you may find jack-in-the pulpit and Indian pipes in the rich, black, damp soil. Turn right up a wooded hillside toward the tracks, then turn left up a rocky trail. Bear left at a trail intersection at .1 mile (the trail to your right is your return route). The trail takes you to Glen Onoko Run, cascading over rocks in a hemlock- and rhododendron-filled ravine.

The trail leads steeply uphill, on both natural and constructed stone steps, but it is eroded away in places. At .2 mile, you are forced to the west side of the stream by steep terrain. A faint arrow on a rock marks the turn to cross on stepping-stones. Just follow the most obvious route up.

Cross again to the east side when the terrain demands it. Here we saw a group of fifth-grade boys and their leaders leaping nimbly about the rocks. Hemlock and white pine are the predominant tree species. The hemlock roots and rocks provide convenient handholds.

Still on the east side, reach the first major falls, 90-foot Onoko Falls. The trail turns up to the right again a short distance to the second major falls, Chameleon Falls, 150 feet high. This is perhaps the most dramatic and colorful of the falls. A broad sheet of water falls over a backdrop of pink, purple, and gray sandstone. It is especially beautiful when the sun is shining. Sheer rock walls on the west side frame the view.

Continue up the steep trail to the top of the falls. Just 20 feet from the drop over the falls, cross to the west side on a flat rock covered with an inch of water flowing over it. Watch your step and any children, and avoid the edge of the falls and that 150-foot drop. There is a fabulous, if vertiginous, view over the top of the falls to the Lehigh River far below.

Again you cross to the east side when the rhododendron becomes impenetrable. Soon you reach the third major falls. Although it is only about 30 feet high, you are able to stand directly behind the falls on a rock ledge without getting wet.

Continue uphill on stone steps to a clearing on a large, flat rock above these falls. (Don't cross the stream again.) The trail continues uphill on stone steps. At the top of the steps, at a stone fire ring, turn right on a rocky, well-worn trail (at 1 mile). There is a faint arrow on a rock pointing the way.

Pitch pine and lichen-covered rocks predominate on the dry ridgeline. The rocky trail goes steadily downhill in a southeasterly direction. About halfway down, a sharp left turn leads back uphill to a view on the Packer Point Trail. The downhill trail swings to a southwesterly direction. Continue down through a young hardwood forest of birch and maple to the railroad tracks. Turn right to follow your return route under the tracks and the access road to reach your car at 2.1 miles.

This hike can be combined with a lazy float down the Lehigh in an inner tube or raft. The Lehigh River is class III white water at peak flow and is popular for white-water sports. Four concessioner outfitters provide transportation, rafts, guides, and equipment for rafting, tubing, kayaking, and canoeing on the river: Whitewater Challengers, 717-443-9532; Pocono Whitewater Adventures, 717-325-3656; Jim Thorpe River Adventures, 717-325-2570; and Whitewater Rafting Adventures, 717-722-0285.

25. HAWK MOUNTAIN SANCTUARY

Distance	6.5 miles
Elevation	820 feet
Time to hike	4¼ hours
Surface	Extremely rocky woods trail, with scrambling over boulders required
Interesting features	Spring and fall raptor migration, views
Facilities	Water, rest rooms at the Visitors Center, which has exhibits and a nature-oriented gift shop; binoculars can be rented at the Visitors Center; picnicking permitted on the lookouts
Hunting	No

Directions

From I-78 (Exit 9) west of Allentown:

1. North on PA 61 for 4.2 miles to PA 895
2. Turn right (east) on PA 895 for 2.4 miles to Hawk Mountain Road
3. Turn right on Hawk Mountain Road (SR 2018) for 1.9 miles to the sanctuary on the right

Coordinates 40°38'02"N; 75°59'15"W

In September, October, and November, during fall color, over 17,000 hawks, eagles, and falcons ride the air currents over the Kittatinny Ridge at Hawk Mountain on their annual migrations. Some travel thousands of miles to southern South America. There are reasons to visit Hawk Mountain at other seasons, too. In April the raptors return. Migrating warblers and waterbirds fly north in May when the dogwood, shadbush, and wildflowers are in bloom. Great rhododendrons bloom in July, and on our last visit in June, mountain and sheep laurel were in glorious pink and white flower. Nonmigrating birds such as owls, woodpeckers, turkeys, and vultures are found at Hawk Mountain all year long.

The sanctuary is privately owned and is open from 9 to 5 every day; from September through November, it is open from 8 to 5. Admission is $4 for adults, $3 for seniors, and $2 for children aged 6 to 12. On weekends from September 1 to November 30, admission fees are slightly higher. (Admission is free to members.)

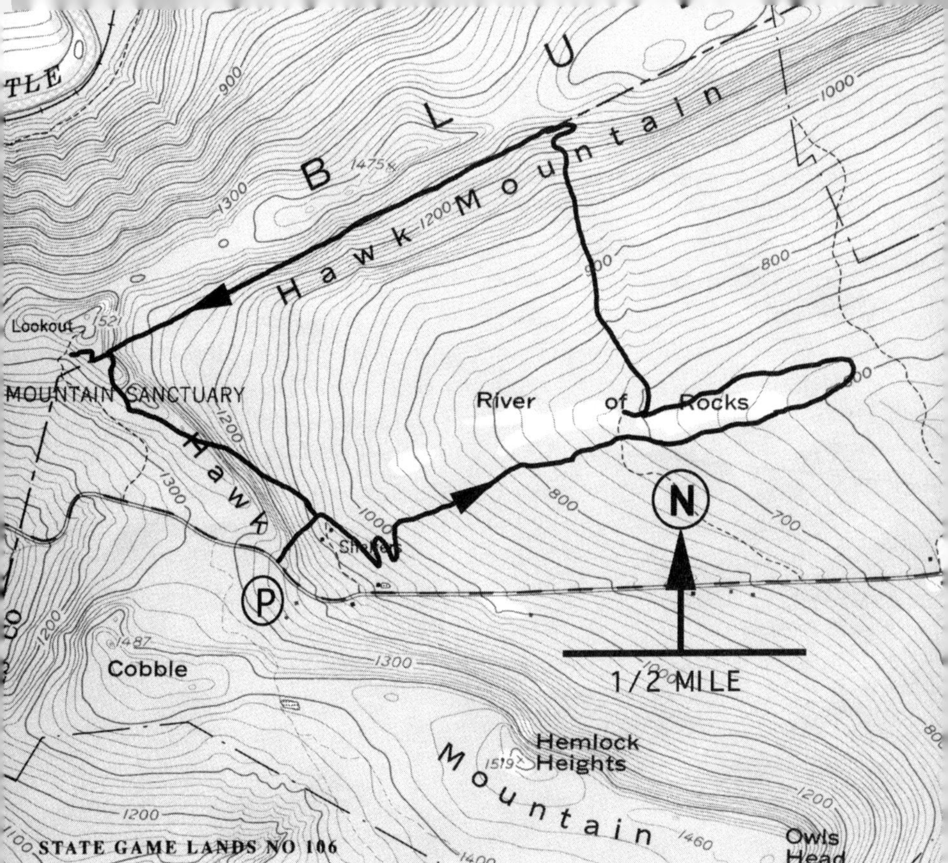

From the Visitors Center, follow the trail as it crosses Hawk Mountain Road and continues past a wire fence "exclosure," built in 1998 to exclude deer. A study of deer impact on the forest is being conducted here. At South Lookout, turn right to follow the red-blazed River of Rocks Trail. The trail soon becomes very rocky as you walk along and through wooded sections of the boulder field. Under the trees, the rocks are greenish gray with lichen. Out in the sun-drenched River of Rocks, they appear almost white. Notice the deep scratches, often in parallel rows, on many of the rocks. These are glacial striations, marks caused by the glacier as it moved over bedrock perhaps 20,000 years ago.

A yellow-blazed trail comes in from the left, but stay on the red-blazed trail beside the River of Rocks. At 2 miles, you round the eastern border of the boulder field in a grove of dense hemlocks and rhododendrons. The so-called Upside Down River, which drains into Kettle Creek, can be heard rushing underneath the rocks.

The trail becomes somewhat less rocky as you follow the red blazes to an intersection with the Golden Eagle Trail. Turn right (north), following the yellow blazes. The ascent up the mountainside becomes steeper and steeper, switchbacking near the top just before an intersection with the blue-blazed Skyline Trail. A right turns here leads to the Appalachian Trail. For this hike, turn left.

The trail climbs up and over piles of jumbled boulders along the ridgeline, and you will be glad you wore your hiking boots. Finally, at East Rocks, you have great views to the north and south. The River of Rocks lies below. North Overlook and the roof of the Visitors Center are farther along the ridge. Few bird watchers venture out here, and you are likely to have the rocks and the vistas to yourself. Pink-colored inclusions in the Tuscarora sandstone are rose quartz.

Rounding a white-and-pink boulder, we came upon a black vulture on a rock less than 20 feet away. Although she appeared a little nervous, she showed no signs of leaving and in fact moved closer. We soon realized why when she ducked into a crevice under a rock, apparently to tend to her nestlings.

The rocks get ever larger. Clinging to the boulders with toe- and handholds, and just when you think the trail can't get any steeper, you climb up to North Lookout. Any number of birders will be studying the sky with binoculars. Join them for a rest and the 200-degree view. On a clear day, you can see 70 miles. Several species of raptors, once hunted nearly to extinction from this overlook, have staged a comeback at Hawk Mountain. Peregrine falcons, golden eagles, and bald eagles are regularly seen during fall and spring migration.

Continue on the orange-blazed trail to a trail sign, then down steep stone steps to a deep hemlock ravine, the "Hall of the Mountain King." Sandstone was mined here in the late nineteenth century. Continue ahead to the "Slide," where the rocks were lowered by an early gravity railroad down the steep north slope to rock crushers at the base of the mountain. A side trail leads to more views to the northwest at Sunset Overlook. The sandy, orange-blazed Scenic Lookout Trail is studded with rocks and leads past four more fine overlooks (with benches) until you again reach South Overlook. Continue ahead to the Visitors Center and your car.

26. LOCUST LAKE STATE PARK

Distance	4 miles
Elevation	300 feet
Time to hike	2 hours
Surface	Rocky woods trail
Interesting features	Scenic stream and lake, tree identification trail
Facilities	Water, rest rooms, picnic facilities around the lake
Hunting	Yes

Directions

From I-81 (Exit 37) north of Pottsville:

1. East on PA 54 for 3.6 miles to SR 1006 (follow signs to Locust Lake State Park)
2. Turn right on SR 1006 for 2 miles to SR 1011
3. Turn left on SR 1011 for 1.5 miles to Locust Lake Road
4. Turn right on Locust Lake Road for .5 mile to the park entrance

Coordinates 40°47'16"N; 76°07'12"W

This short and pretty hike is ideal for families. Kids can hunt for crayfish, frogs, and salamanders along the stream. Older folks find it a fairly easy walk, which can be shortened at several points. The park includes 1,144 acres and a picturesque lake of 52 acres in a deep valley close to the headwaters of Locust Creek. It is heavily wooded, with dense hemlock and mountain laurel along the stream and a variety of hardwoods at higher elevations. Deer, wild turkeys, and squirrels are abundant in the park.

Begin your hike at the day-use parking lot to the right, just before the park entrance. Walk past the small camp office, where you can pick up a trail map. Continue south across the impoundment between Locust Lake and a small pond at the bottom of the spillway. Just past a boat launch area, you find the paved bicycle trail that completely circles the lake. In summer, Locust Lake is a popular camping area, especially for families with children. The lake offers a small swimming beach, a playground, environmental programs, boat rentals, and fishing.

The bicycle trail winds past campsites through mature hemlocks and mountain laurel, the state flower. At .5 mile, you reach a small amphitheater, and just after that, a large trail sign, the beginning of the 5-mile trail system. For the longest route, follow the white blazes. You can shorten the hike by turning right at any trail intersection for a shorter loop.

The trail follows Locust Creek, a pretty little stream that tumbles over rocks through quiet woodland. After crossing a wooden bridge, you pick up the Tree Discovery Trail, an Eagle Scout project constructed in 1995. Small posts identify twenty-one types of trees and vegetation along the trail. At .7 mile, the blue-blazed Ridge Trail and the tree identification posts turn right. Continue ahead on

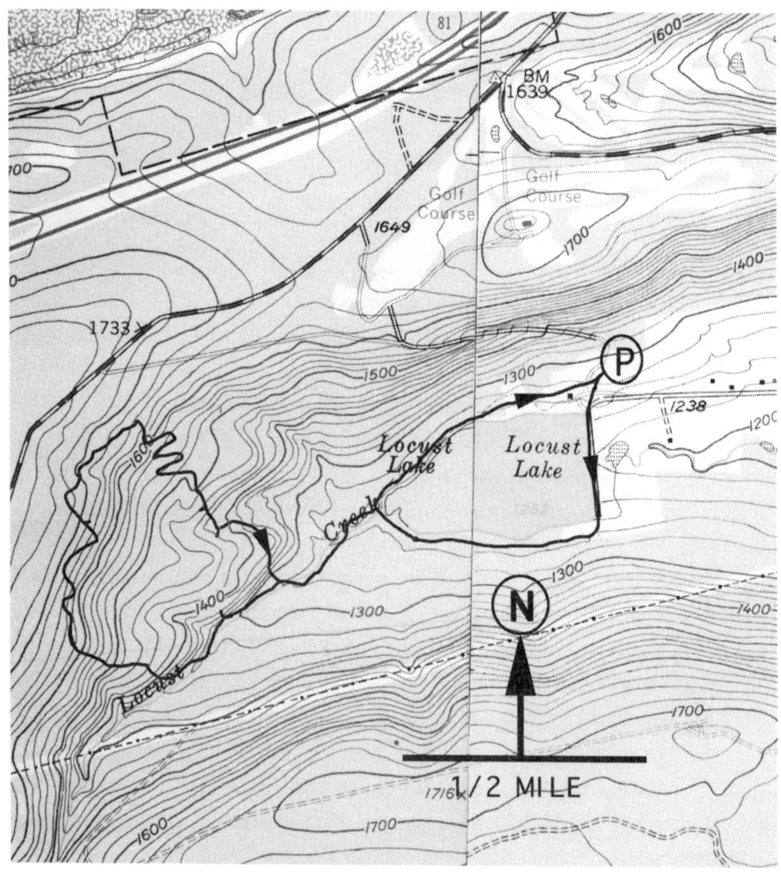

White-tailed deer

the white-blazed trail, crossing the stream twice on rocks or logs. In high water, you may get your feet wet.

The trail turns uphill, leaving the stream bank. The hemlocks give way to mixed oaks and hickories at a rock outcropping. A yellow-blazed trail comes in from the right; continue ahead on the white-blazed trail. Soon the trail steepens on a series of switchbacks to the top of a ridgeline at 2.1 miles.

There was evidence of a fire here, which cleared out the understory and small shrubs but only scorched the trunks and lower branches of the larger trees. In early spring, there were already signs of regeneration, with skunk cabbage and small wildflowers emerging from the forest floor.

Descend from the ridge on switchbacks. A yellow-blazed trail and then the blue-blazed trail come in from the right, and you pick up more tree identification posts. At the wooden bridge, you begin to retrace your steps to the bicycle trail. Turn left here to continue around the lake on the bicycle path and return to the parking lot and your car.

PART THREE

SUSQUEHANNA RIVER VALLEY

Luzerne and Lackawanna Counties

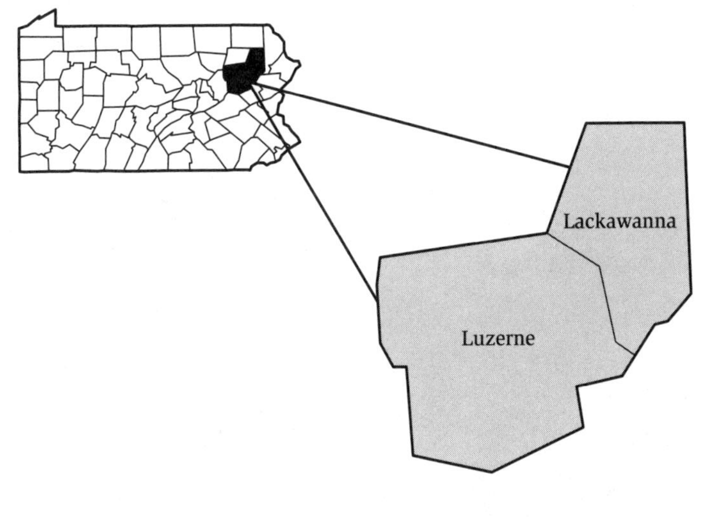

27. LAKE SCRANTON

Distance	3.7 miles
Elevation	50 feet
Time to hike	1½ hours
Surface	Asphalt path circling the lake
Interesting features	Views of lake
Facilities	Benches
Hunting	No

Directions

From I-81 (Exit 52, Moosic Street) east of Scranton: south on PA 307 for 1.8 miles to parking lot on the right

Coordinates 41°23'20"N; 75°37'17"W

Lake Scranton is owned and operated by Pennsylvania American Water Company for the water supply of Scranton. The trail is accessible to everyone and is popular with joggers and families with strollers. Chipmunks and squirrels are quite tame and approach you looking for a handout. No picnicking, water sports, bicycles, pets, or exploring off trail is permitted.

Merganser

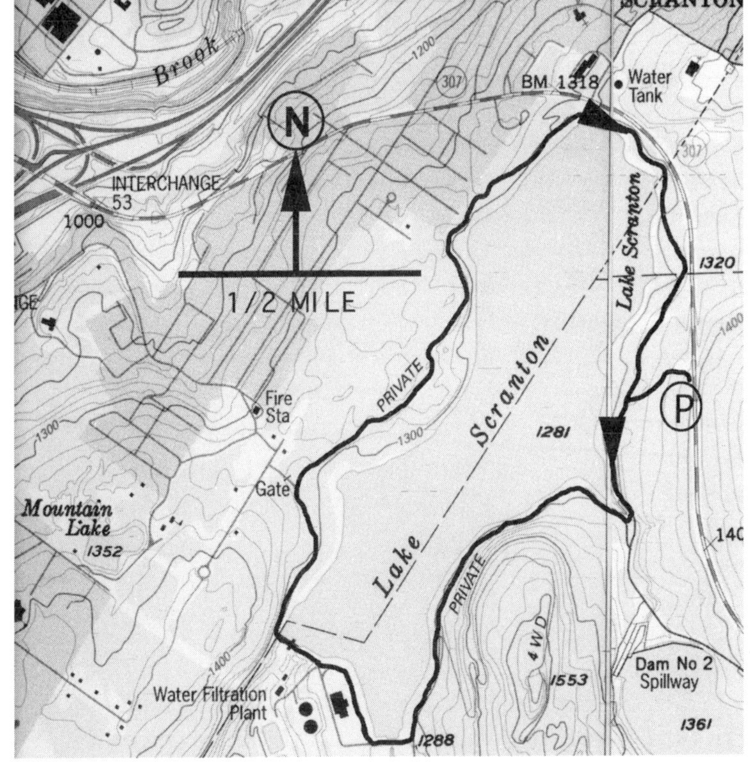

Walk down from the parking lot on a gravel path, either the Hemlock Trail or the Stonewall Trail, to the asphalt trail. We turned left, but you could go in either direction. Mileages in either direction are painted on the path.

At .4 mile, you cross a bridge, then turn right on Lake Scranton Road. You are requested to stay to the right on the pedestrian walkway for the next mile. Hemlocks and red pines give way to mixed hardwoods, oaks, scrub maples, and birches at the water's edge.

Cross a backwater on a bridge. You are likely to see pintails, mallards, or mergansers in the water. At 1.5 miles, you leave the road at several water facility buildings. Stay on the asphalt path, which shortly crosses a stone bridge at the water intake just before the Old Scranton Gas and Water Building.

At 1.6 miles, you pass a handicapped-accessible fishing pier, gazebo, and picnic table. There is an adjoining wheelchair-accessible parking lot available by permission. Contact Allied Services at 717-348-1332 for information.

Pass stone row fences. At 3 miles, pass lake overlooks at a pier. At 3.6 miles, you complete the loop; follow the gravel path to return to your car at 3.7 miles.

28. LACKAWANNA STATE PARK

Distance	5.5 miles
Elevation	560 feet
Time to hike	3 hours
Surface	Rocky woods trail that may be muddy
Interesting features	Farmland in colonial times, now second-growth forest; old stone rows; old pine and hemlock plantation
Facilities	Rest rooms, picnic facilities at the start of Abington Riding Trail (at .3 mile)
Hunting	Yes

Directions

From I-81 (Exit 60) north of Scranton:

1. West on PA 524 for 3.2 miles (pass the park office at 3 miles) to PA 407
2. Turn left (south) on PA 407 for .4 mile to access road
3. Turn sharply right, pass a boat mooring area, and continue .4 mile to the parking lot by the lake

Coordinates 41°33'33"N; 76°42'23"W

Lackawanna State Park is notable for the various stages of field succession and forest regeneration you can observe. Open meadows alternate with second-growth woods and overgrown conifer plantations. Crisscrossing the hillsides with stone row fences, nineteenth-century farmers cultivated fields and orchards at lower elevations. Pine and hemlock trees were planted in neat rows on rockier mountainsides.

Walk back on the road you drove in on, past picnic facilities and a boat mooring area along the lake. Turn right on the Abington Riding Trail just before reaching PA 407. Cross a wooden bridge over States Creek. Look just upstream of the bridge; we saw a beaver dam that has flooded the entire area. At a trail intersection, turn left.

The trail leads uphill. Cross a power-line cut at .5 mile, and then turn right near the top of a rise, entering an old hemlock and pine plantation. The trail winds through mixed evergreens. Watch closely for the orange blazes and ribbons tied at rider's eye level that mark the riding trail.

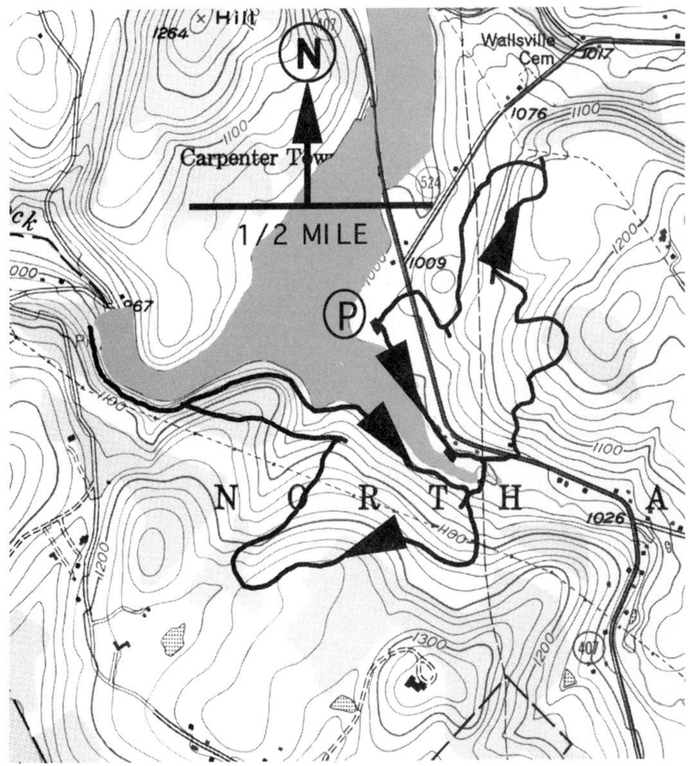

The evergreens give way to mixed hardwoods as you follow the park boundary. If you look closely, you may see the foundation remains of an old farmhouse. After crossing a power-line cut at a stone row fence, the trail leads downhill to the Frost Hollow Trail. Turn left, following blue diamonds nailed to trees. Bear left on the Snowflake Trail at 2.3 miles.

The trail leads beside the lake, crossing a stream on stepping-stones. At 2.5 miles, you reach the Lackawanna dam and spillway. Retrace your steps, this time bearing left at the trail intersection, remaining on the Snowflake Trail at 2.7 miles.

The trail is marked with yellow diamonds nailed to trees and is muddy in the spring. A stone row fence, built and abandoned before the Tunkhannock Creek was dammed in 1969–70, leads directly into the lake. At 3.6 miles, you reach the road. Turn right and then cross PA 407. Pick up the Abington Trail beside the park sign.

The trail leads steeply uphill through more stone rows. Soon, second-growth hardwoods give way to old orchards. Nesting boxes at the edges of open fields attract bluebirds. The Bluebird Trails Project of the Department of Conservation and Natural Resources (DCNR) is run by volunteers who construct and erect the boxes at various places in the park. There are about 1,500 nest boxes in fifty-seven state parks throughout Pennsylvania. The volunteers monitor them throughout the spring, summer, and fall, counting the number of nests, eggs, and baby birds. This research will assist the DCNR in improving the habitat of bluebirds.

Turn right at a T intersection with the Turkey Hill Trail, marked with yellow diamonds. The trail leads steeply uphill to views of farmland to the east. Bear left at a Y intersection to stay on the trail marked with yellow diamonds.

After completing the Turkey Hill Loop at a wooden bridge, the trail returns to PA 407. Cross the road to a grassy path just beside the guardrail. Continue straight ahead to the parking lot and your car.

There are other trails described in the park recreation guide, which you can pick up at the park office.

29. SEVEN TUBS NATURE AREA

Distance	2.6 miles
Elevation	240 feet
Time to hike	1¼ hours
Surface	First .2 mile, paved asphalt trail and wooden bridge; then rocky trail
Interesting features	Scenic stream and "tubs" through a hemlock gorge, mountain views from the top of a ridge
Facilities	Picnic tables at parking areas
Hunting	Yes

Directions

From I-81 (Exit 47) near Wilkes-Barre:

1. South on PA 115 for 1.5 miles to park entrance road
2. Turn right into park entrance for .2 mile to parking lot on the left
3. For handicapped parking, continue .1 mile to parking lot on the right

Coordinates 41°14'09"N; 75°48'28"W

At the Seven Tubs Nature Area, glacial meltwater created a series of potholes in an area now called Whirlpool Valley. Maintained by Luzerne County in State Game Lands 292, this lovely hike is notable for these glacial "tubs," or pools, which waterfalls continue to carve and deepen through bedrock.

From the regular parking lot, walk down the road to the handicapped parking area on the right. Opposite is the start of the paved trail, which winds along the bank of Wheelbarrow Run and then crosses it on a 60-foot wooden bridge. From here you can look up and down the hemlock gorge to see the first two tubs at the base of 5-foot falls. Five more tubs and falls continue upstream to your left.

Turn left just before the bridge to follow yellow blazes painted on trees and rocks. To your right is a steep ravine, carved into sandstone of the Pocono formation by Wheelbarrow Run. Narrow crevasses separate the falls and potholes, the largest 30 feet across. The rocky, dry ridge above the stream has been swept by periodic fires.

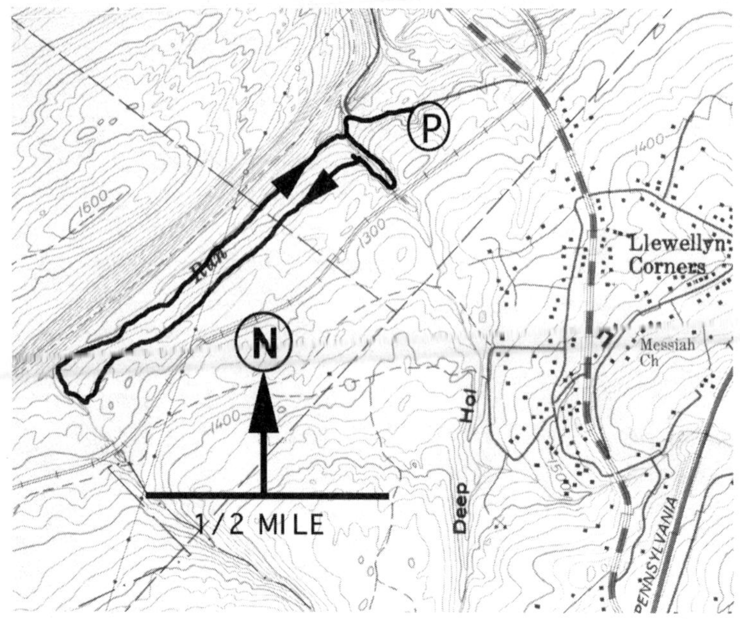

Pitch pine, scrub oak, and red maple are able to regenerate, and new growth sprouts from burned trunks.

A ship ladder descends into the ravine. Here the temperature is much cooler, and eastern hemlock, mountain holly, and laurel predominate, unaffected by fires at the higher elevations. At .5 mile, cross Wheelbarrow Run on a wooden bridge and turn right (north) on the west side of the stream.

The surface, covered with pine needles and rocks, is slippery in places and rises steeply, with the stream well below you. (You can shorten the hike to 1 mile by continuing straight ahead, then turning right at the wooden bridge to return to the parking lot.)

Just after a large rock at .7 mile, watch for double blue blazes of the Audubon Trail. Turn left sharply uphill (west), following the blue-blazed trail to the top of the ridge. Here the surface becomes very rocky, and the vegetation thins out again to scrub pines, oaks, and blueberries. From the top of the ridge, you have fine views of the surrounding countryside to the east and south.

Walk west and reach a more thickly wooded area of small birches, oaks, sassafras, and witch hazel. Pink azaleas bloom here in April. At

1.1 miles, reach a power-line cut running north-south. The blue blazes (on rocks) cross the cut and reenter the woods on the other side, continuing west.

At 1.3 miles, reach and cross a faint woods road. Continue straight ahead on the blue-blazed trail. The trail turns downhill, crosses a small stream on stepping-stones, then turns uphill again. The direction turns to the southwest. Cross another indistinct woods road.

Continue straight ahead on the blue-blazed trail and reach a small, unnamed stream at 1.8 miles. Turn right (north), downstream along the picturesque stream through hemlocks and mountain and sheep laurel. The gorge steepens on both sides. The small stream joins Laurel Run and turns east. At 2.1 miles, pass a very large rock, 10 feet high and 30 feet wide. The trail climbs up out of the gorge on a bare rock outcropping in a clearing, and then back down again.

Laurel Run widens as you cross several more tributaries. At 2.2 miles, the water rushes through a gap in the rocks and down a 15-foot-high fall to a deep, clear pool 30 feet across. Laurel Run converges with Wheelbarrow Run, sliding over a 30-foot-wide, 40-foot-long, smooth rock slab. Turn right uphill to the bridge and cross over it to retrace your steps to your car at 2.6 miles.

The Seven Tubs Nature Area is open daily from 8 A.M. to sunset from May 15 to September 15. In early spring and fall, it is open only on weekends. We recommend a call to the Luzerne County parks office at 717-477-5467 between September and May to make sure the park is open when you plan to visit.

30. FRANCES SLOCUM STATE PARK

Distance	7.2 miles
Elevation	400 feet
Time to hike	3½ hours
Surface	Woods road, mown path through fields, rocky trail
Interesting features	The story of five-year-old Frances Slocum and her abduction by Lenapes, historic nineteenth-century stone row fences, large red pine plantation
Facilities	Water, rest rooms, picnic tables, grills at lake-side and picnic areas
Hunting	Yes

Directions

From US 11 north of Wilkes-Barre:

1. North on PA 309 (toward Luzerne-Dallas) for 3.3 miles to Carverton Road
2. Turn right on Carverton Road (SR 1036) for 4.2 miles to a T intersection—West Eighth Street
3. Turn left on West Eighth Street (SR 1021) for 1.3 miles to Mount Olivet Road
4. Turn left on Mount Olivet Road (SR 1044) for .9 mile to park entrance road
5. Turn left on park entrance road for .9 mile (passing the park office at .3 mile)
6. At a T intersection, turn right at a sign for the boat rental area; continue .1 mile to the parking lot beside the lake

Coordinates 41°20'10"N; 75°53'33"W

The park is named for Frances Slocum, a young Quaker girl who was kidnapped by Indians. Frances was one of nine children of Mr. and Mrs. Jonathan Slocum. On November 2, 1778, while the men were at work in the fields, a war party of Lenapes entered the Slocum farmhouse, located in what is now Wilkes-Barre. They carried away five-year-old Frances to a hiding place under a rock ledge near Abrahams Creek, which provided some shelter from the cold. During the night, the girl tried to escape but was soon recaptured. The Lenapes renamed Frances Weletawash.

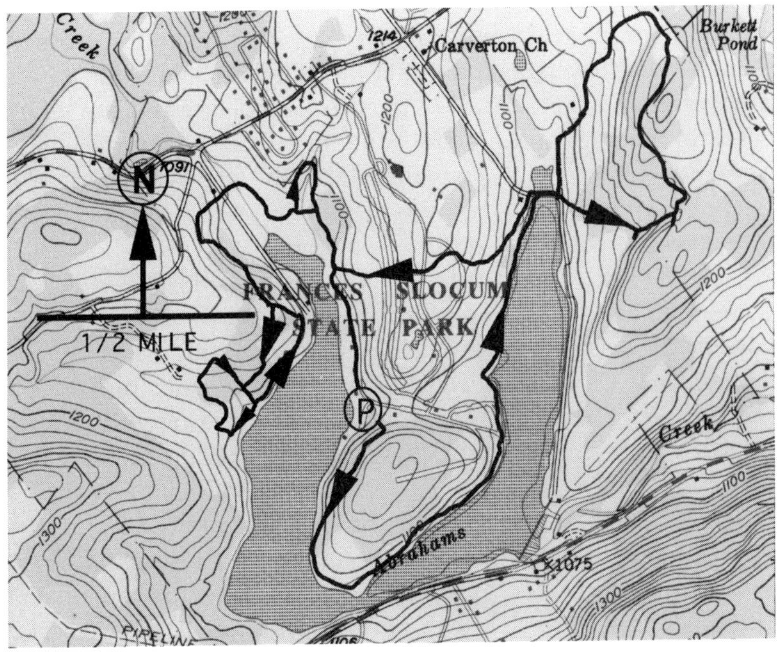

Frances accompanied the Lenapes as they moved westward. Later, she married into the Miami tribe and was given the name Mocanaquah, meaning "young bear." Her family never gave up the search for her. Fifty-nine years after her kidnapping, her brothers found her living on a reservation in New Reserve, Indiana. She had been married twice to chieftains and had four children. Mocanaquah told her story to her brothers but refused to return to her childhood home in Pennsylvania. She died at the age of seventy-four and was buried in Indiana.

The trailhead for the Frances Slocum Trail is at the edge of the woods, opposite the lake. The blue-blazed trail leads uphill on a hemlock- and pine-covered slope. At .1 mile, reach a rock shelter at the base of a 40-foot cliff. This is the site where the Indians held little Frances overnight, near Abrahams Creek (now Frances Slocum Lake). The rocky cliff continues on the left, the lake on the right.

At .3 mile, bear right on the red-blazed Lakeshore Trail. The trail continues along the lake on a wide, grassy road, which soon enters an old pine plantation. At 1.1 miles, leave the woods for a grassy field along the lake at a pier and boat mooring area. Continue to follow the red blazes past picnic pavilion 3.

Walk through a mown area 10 feet wide through tall grasses. Summer wildflowers, including black-eyed Susan, milkweed, thistle, and butter and eggs, attract butterflies. Red blazes are painted on rocks in the path and on occasional trees. Cattails, rushes, wild grapes, and sumac grow along the edge of the lake. When you reach the point where the trail reenters the woods, you'll notice the extensive damage to trees by beavers.

At 1.5 miles, you reach the northern end of the lake. The Lakeshore Trail ends at a camp access road. Cross the lake inlet on the road over a culvert. Notice a yellow gate on the left, which is your return route. Continue straight ahead for 25 feet, then turn left off the road to follow the double orange blazes of the Larch Tree Trail. The trail leads uphill (southeast) through a mixed hardwood forest along an old stone row fence.

The Larch Tree Trail continues on an old woods road to the eastern boundary of the park. There are several intersecting trails; stay with the orange blazes. At 2.5 miles, you reach the top of a hill and the vegetation thins out, with many blueberries, scrub oaks, and shrubs. American larch (tamarack), a deciduous conifer, can be identified by its soft pinelike needles that turn yellow in the fall and its rough, scaly bark.

There is a stone row fence along the property line. At 2.7 miles, you reach a large, abandoned red pine plantation and walk through it for a quarter mile. It is very quiet, with little other vegetation or wildlife. At 3.5 miles, you pass more larches and again reach the yellow gate, the road, and the northern end of the lake. Continue across the lake inlet, then walk uphill on the camp access road on the left side facing traffic. At 3.6 miles, reach the top of the hill and turn left through an opening between a wooden guardrail and a stone row fence. Proceed across a mown field for 150 feet along the edge of the woods to the main park road at picnic area 2. Turn left, walking 100 feet toward a large water tower. Turn right at a service road, pass a lower parking lot, and continue straight ahead to a field.

Walk straight ahead across the field toward picnic tables and a water pump between a gully and a line of paper birch trees to the left. Enter the woods and walk 600 feet west to a yellow-blazed trail beside an old pine tree at 4 miles. Turn left at a trail intersection on the nature trail, cross a stream, and reach another large, old white pine at a wooden post. Turn left.

Paper birch

The trail is blazed yellow. At 4.1 miles, you cross a rocky streambed in a hemlock and pine forest. The trail rises to reach a meadow reverting to woods, with 10-foot-high shrubs on both sides. At a clearing, cross Abrahams Creek (another inlet to the lake) on a wooden footbridge. Continue, crossing an overgrown asphalt road (which predates the lake and leads into it) through mixed hardwoods. The trail leads downhill to reach the lake at 4.7 miles and then immediately turns right to go uphill again.

Walk through another pine plantation on a hillside. You are soon walking through woods crisscrossed with well-constructed nineteenth-century stone row fences. After passing through the third stone fence, you reach a trail intersection (this is the starting point of a figure-eight double loop).

Turn right uphill along the fence. Soon you reach two parallel stone rows. Turn left between them to the edge of the lake, and then turn right. Pass the site of an old stone dam and filled-in farm pond at 5.4 miles. The trail leads uphill. From here you can look across a network of 4-foot-high stone fences, constructed with painstaking effort by nineteenth-century farmers. These fences are especially well built, and most are in good condition. Rocks are layered horizontally, then topped by a row of vertically placed rocks, all without benefit of mortar. The number of fences in this area suggests that they were used to enclose farm animals. Look for Indian pipes in the moist soil near the stone rows. Descend the rocky cliff on stone steps.

Return to the double stone rows and retrace your steps to the lake. This time, turn left along the lake, still following the yellow blazes. A stone fence leads directly into the lake. At the next fence row, complete the figure-eight double loop. Retrace your steps through the pine plantation.

Cross the asphalt road again and retrace your steps back to the footbridge over Abrahams Creek at 6.2 miles. Continue straight ahead at a wood post and old pine on the Nature Trail. Cross a rocky stream through hemlocks and rhododendrons, then through mixed hardwoods and pines, completing the Nature Trail Loop. Continue to a grassy clearing near the lake. Walk toward the Nature Center building (open Saturday and Sunday, 1 to 5 P.M.) and reach the parking lot at 7.2 miles.

31. NESCOPECK PONDS LOOP

Distance	3.2 miles
Elevation	165 feet
Time to hike	1½ hours
Surface	Grassy woods road, rocky trail
Interesting features	Two beaver ponds, Lake Nescopeck
Facilities	None
Hunting	Yes

Directions

From I-80 (Exit 39) south of Wilkes-Barre:

1. South on PA 309 for .9 mile to Honey Hole Road (no street sign; a Country Corners Citgo station is on the right)
2. Left on Honey Hole Road for 5.2 miles (pass under I-80) to game-lands parking area on the right. (There is an asphalt road .1 mile farther on the right, adjacent to a building. This is the unmarked entrance to Nescopeck State Park. If you miss the turn, turn around here and backtrack to the game-lands parking area.)

Coordinates 41°05'06"N; 75°53'12"W

This is a short, scenic hike through State Game Lands 187 and the undeveloped 2,981-acre Nescopeck State Park. The trail takes you to two beaver dams and Nescopeck Lake. The recreational lake was created for a housing development in the early 1970s and was acquired by the state in 1990; there are still a few occupied homes near the lake. There are plans to develop Nescopeck into an environmental center and campground. For now, the park is managed by the State Game Commission. The trail is not blazed, but it is fairly easy to follow on wide, grassy woods roads and lake and pond loop trails.

From the parking area, walk around a metal gate to a gravel, then grassy woods road. The road is just below Nescopeck Lake, which is out of view to the left, across a marshy area below the dam. The road crosses the dam outlet on a culvert through mixed hardwoods. Notice a faint trail coming in from your left just after the dam—this will be your return route. Continue straight ahead.

Just after a forest cut at .4 mile, bear left at a Y intersection with another grassy woods road. At .8 mile, pass pines; then you will hear

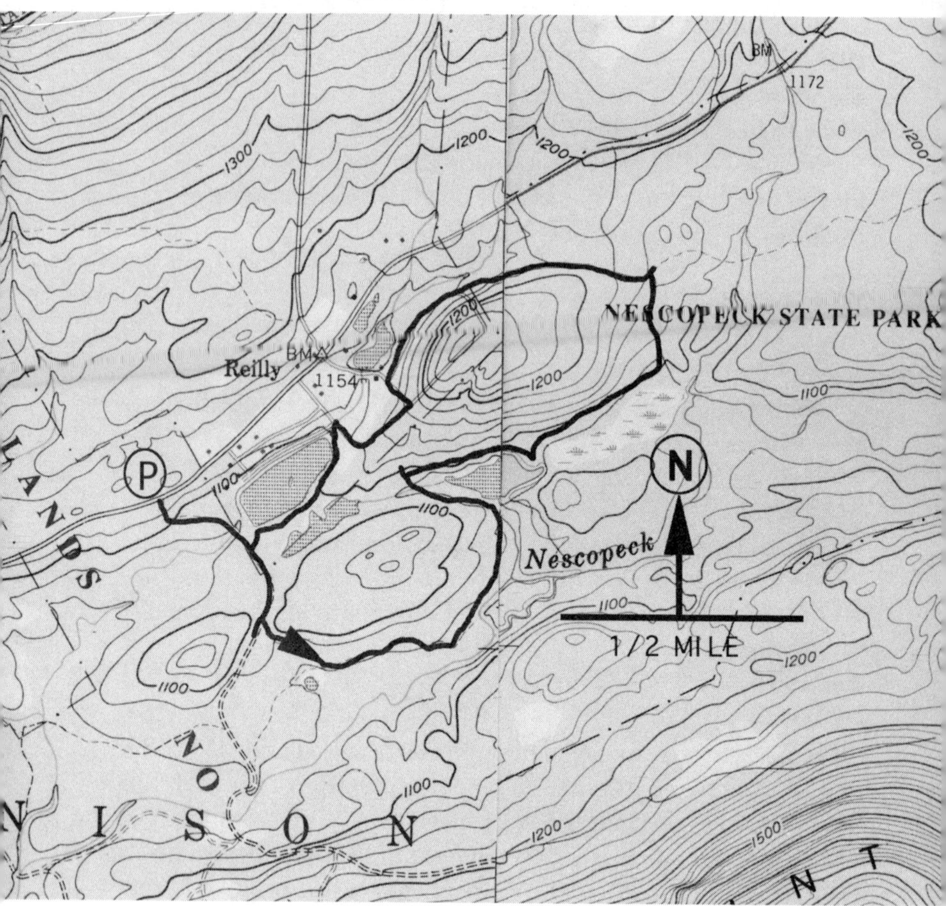

a stream rushing off to your right. A short side trail leads through hemlocks to Nescopeck Creek. Return to the woods road, which parallels the stream a short distance, then continues up a rise to a rock-strewn area of sparse scrubby trees.

Pass a rock outcropping. Just before a large pond, turn left on a well-defined though unblazed woods trail. The trail follows the edge of the shallow beaver pond. Cross a small stream on sticks (a dry wash in late summer) between a smaller pond on your left and the one on your right.

Five hundred feet after crossing the stream, a faint path between the two ponds crosses the trail. (If you continue straight ahead, the trail leads to the upper end of Nescopeck Lake, for a total hike of 1.7 miles.) For this hike, turn right (east), to walk along the edge of the first pond. Several wood-duck nesting boxes are placed in the trees along the water. You have a view of Mount Yeager across the shallow pond, dotted with tree stumps.

At the beaver dam, turn left (north) at a T intersection with a grassy woods road. Cattails, willows, and rushes fill a marsh and clearing on your right just beyond the line of trees.

The trail continues to a T intersection with another grassy road. A right turn would lead down to Nescopeck Creek. Instead, turn left (north), uphill through young birches, aspens, and sassafras. Pass two grassy roads on the right. The road turns to the west around the hill. When you reach the top of the rise, pass a woods road on the left. At the *second* woods road from the left, at 2 miles, turn left (south).

There are a few pink ribbons tied to trees. The road ends and becomes a trail in a dark hemlock grove. A white metal post marks the boundary between the game lands and the state park ahead. The trail is initially well defined along a hemlock slope, then a little more difficult through briers and field reverting to forest. Very soon the trail ends and continues as a red gravel road. There are piles of creosote timbers along the road, apparently taken up when railroad trestle tracks were removed. Pass a large abandoned barn on your right. At a T intersection and another abandoned farm building, turn left uphill on a moss-covered asphalt road.

At the top of a hill at 2.7 miles, turn right at another T intersection. Just before a metal gate, turn left on a trail toward the upper end of Nescopeck Lake. The mixed hardwoods thin out to scrub oaks, paper birches, and junipers in the rocky, sandy soil. Follow the trail to the left around the lake. Just before you reach the earthen dam, turn left (south) on a trail. The trail takes you through a rocky field, then back to the grassy road where you began the loop. Turn right and retrace your steps to return to your car.

32. RIVERSIDE COMMONS

Distance	2.5 miles
Elevation	30 feet
Time to hike	1¼ hours
Surface	Gravel, asphalt, and wood-chipped path
Interesting features	Floodplain ecology, Susquehanna River
Facilities	Picnic tables, benches (tables, grills, water, Jiffy John at Kirby Park)
Hunting	No

Directions

From I-81 (Exit 47) near Wilkes-Barre:

1. North on PA 309 for 3 miles to Exit 4 (Kingston–Forty Fort)
2. Turn left on Rutter Avenue for .1 mile to Church Street
3. Left on Church Street for .4 mile
4. Bear right on 3rd Avenue for 1.2 miles
5. Turn left on Market Street for .1 mile
6. Turn right into Kirby Park for .2 mile to parking lot at large trail sign

From Town Square in Wilkes-Barre: west on Market Street for .6 mile to Kirby Park on your left

Coordinates 41°15'02"N; 75°53'34"W

The Riverside Trails at Kirby and Nesbitt Parks explore the wide floodplain of the Susquehanna River and the dikes built in the late 1930s to protect the west-side communities of Wyoming, Forty Fort, Kingston, and Edwardsville from floods. The Susquehanna River, translated as "River of Winding Shore" or "Muddy River," has been designated a heritage river by the federal government.

Park at the large trail map at Kirby Park. (This map overstates actual distances.) Turn right and follow the asphalt path past crab-apple trees and a volleyball court. Bear left at swings on a gravel path between the 30-foot-high dike and the tennis courts. When you reach the top of the dike, continue straight ahead on the Olmsted Trail.

The Olmsted Trail becomes a wide, asphalt path. Short trails to the right lead to the Warriors Path, which more closely follows the river edge. Follow either the Olmsted Trail or Warriors Path east

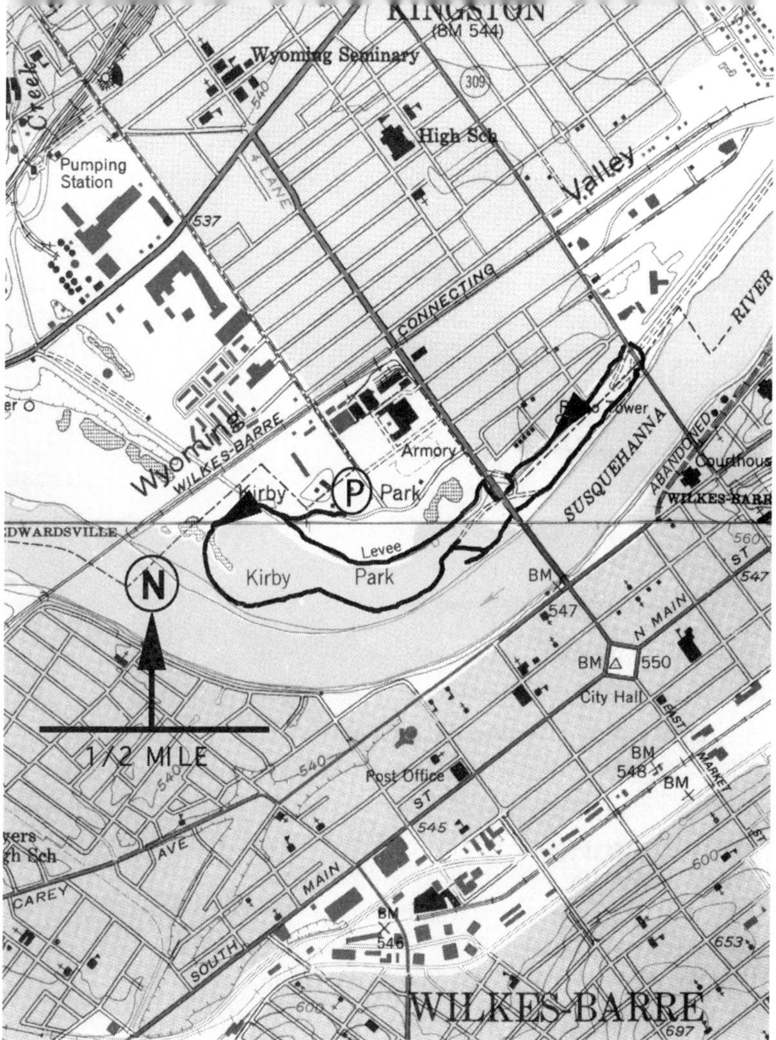

between the dike and the river. Jumbled concrete blocks along the river bear witness to early efforts to contain the Susquehanna. The beach, up to 30 feet wide, is composed of smooth, rounded stones and pebbles.

Large trees with extensive root systems predominate in the fine silt and sand soils of the floodplain. Most common is the silver maple; the leaves have a characteristic silver-colored underside. You will also find red maple, cottonwood, American elm, and shagbark hickory. Vines such as wild grape and poison ivy grow high into the trees. Jewelweed, or "touch-me-not," up to 8 feet high, is covered with yellow and orange flowers in late summer. The showy purple flower on stalks is purple loosestrife, a European native that has become common along many Pennsylvania streams and rivers. Snakes and snapping turtles are the main year-round residents.

Kirby Park was designed by the Olmsted brothers in 1922. A zoo exhibited monkeys, bears, and buffalo. Gardens, a pavilion, a band shell, and an amphitheater were built; then a major flood in 1936 swept everything away. Concrete foundations of many of these structures, including the animal pens, remain. The area was abandoned and vandalized until just a few years ago. Thanks to volunteer efforts, the park is being reclaimed.

At .5 mile, the Olmsted Trail and Warriors Path come together at a restored wading pool, a flower garden, and the foundation of the Gardener's Cottage at a commemorative sign. A concrete wall of the cottage still stands, decorated with leafy vines and inscribed with the words "Susquehanna Mother of Rivers." Plans are under way to rebuild the pavilion for concerts and picnics. Floodproof benches and picnic tables surround the area and overlook the river.

The path continues through a natural meadow filled with a spiny, 6-foot-high thistle called teasel. Queen Anne's lace, field daisies, and goldenrod also fill the meadow in season. The trail leads under the historic Market Street bridge, built in 1929, to Nesbitt Park. Cross a parking lot to an expanse of grassy parkland with large sycamores, river birches, and alders alongside the river. A boat ramp crosses the path. You have a fine view of the river and the dome of the Luzerne County Courthouse.

At 1.3 miles, walk on a road closed to traffic under the Veterans Memorial Bridge. The original bridge, built in 1888, was destroyed in the flood of 1972, caused by Tropical Storm Agnes. The road curves around to Pierce Street. Carefully cross busy Pierce Street to walk back toward Kirby Park on the dike.

A project that has raised the dike an average of 5 feet from Wyoming to Edwardsville is nearly finished. The levee from the Veterans Memorial Bridge to Market Street Bridge is the last section to be completed. The work is being done by the U.S. Corps of Engineers and private contractors.

At Market Street, follow the trail down under the bridge, then up steps to Kirby Park. The asphalt trail around the lake to your

Queen Anne's lace

right is a favorite place for jogging and family outings. There is a large resident population of relatively tame ducks and geese. Great blue herons and peregrine falcons are also often sighted.

You always find a cool breeze on the elevated dike, between grassy ball fields on your right and the Kirby Park Natural Area on your left. The river still regularly inundates the floodplain, occasionally triggering emergency evacuations, but the water has not gone over the dikes since Tropical Storm Agnes. A spillway passing under the dike between the two areas allows water to flow back to the river during times of heavy rainfall.

At 2.3 miles, you complete the loop on the dike. You could continue on the dike for another .3 mile to the Black Diamond Railroad Bridge. Retrace your steps to return to your car.

33. RICKETTS GLEN STATE PARK

Distance	6.8 miles
Elevation	1,150 feet
Time to hike	4 hours
Surface	Narrow, rocky trail along edge of stream, very slippery in places; narrow stone and wooden steps
Interesting features	Lovely hemlock gorge; more than twenty-two named waterfalls, the highest, 94-foot Ganoga Falls
Facilities	Rest rooms, water, picnic facilities at PA 118 and at the park office at Lake Jean
Hunting	No

Directions

From US 11 in Wilkes-Barre:

1. North on PA 309 for 5.8 miles to PA 415
2. PA 309 veers right; continue straight ahead (north) on PA 415 for 2.2 miles
3. Turn left (west) on PA 118 for 16 miles; turn left into parking lot for Ricketts Glen State Park

Coordinates 41°17'54"N; 76°16'33"W

If you like waterfalls, you will enjoy Ricketts Glen. Ganoga Glen and Glen Leigh, tributaries of Kitchen Creek, have cut deep gorges through shale and sandstone rock layers, tumbling over more than twenty-two named and several unnamed waterfalls. The streams converge at Waters Meet and then flow through Ricketts Glen over three additional falls.

The state park is named for Colonel Robert Bruce Ricketts, who served in the Union Army at the Battle of Gettysburg in 1861. Colonel Ricketts owned or controlled 80,000 acres in the area. Through acquisitions from his heirs and additional purchases, the park now encompasses 13,050 acres and is one of the largest parks in Pennsylvania.

To begin the hike, cross PA 118 to the sign reading, "Glen Entrance." Start walking north on the west side of Kitchen Creek

Campground
Lake Rose
RICKETTS GLEN STATE PARK
2200
2100
Leigh
TRAIL
Ganoga
Glen
JEEP
Glen
Kitchen
TRAIL
1800
1900
Shingle Cabin
Maple Spring
Br
N
1600
JEEP
1/2 MILE
1700
Creek
1400
1500
FAIRMOUNT
1700
1800
Picnic Area
1269
Kitchen Creek Falls
Run
P
Boston
1400
1306

through a deeply shaded forest of majestic hemlocks. At .2 mile, you reach a new large trail map, which clearly shows the Y-shaped trail system. A sign warns of the danger in hiking past Waters Meet during the winter and after heavy rains. Many people have been injured and even killed in falls due to slippery conditions.

After crossing Kitchen Creek twice on sturdy wooden bridges, the trail heads uphill away from the creek on a relocation. You rejoin the creek at 1.5 miles at a small tributary, Shingle Cabin Brook, and reach the first falls, the 16-foot Murray Reynolds. Walking along the creek, you shortly encounter the 36-foot Sheldon Reynolds and the 27-foot Harrison Wright. Many of the magnificent pines, hemlocks, and oaks in this area are over 500 years old, and ring counts on fallen trees have revealed ages as high as 900 years. Some trees have diameters of 5 feet and tower over 100 feet high.

You reach Waters Meet at 1.8 miles. Another large sign shows the trail system, as well as each of the named falls and its height. Here Kitchen Creek and the trail both divide.

Turn right to cross Ganoga Glen on a narrow footbridge with a single railing to walk along the west side of Glen Leigh. There are eight falls on this tributary, the highest 41 feet (Huron). The falls are named after relatives of Colonel Ricketts and various Indian tribes. In places, the path is very narrow and continually wet from springs arising from the rock layers, and there are drops of 75 feet or more to the stream below. Your usual hiking pace may be slowed because of the steepness of the climb and the slippery conditions. In winter, the water freezes, making the path unsafe. Be sure to wear sturdy hiking boots and stick to the trail when hiking. Taking shortcuts further increases erosion and can be dangerous.

At the top of the gorge, leave the Glen Leigh Trail to turn left on the Highland Trail. In a few moments, you will be surprised how quiet it becomes as you leave the noisy waterfalls. You can once again carry on a conversation. The trail leads gradually uphill and is often muddy. At 3.7 miles, you walk through a gap in some immense 30-foot-high conglomerate boulders at Midway Crevasse. At 4 miles, turn left on the Ganoga Glen Trail (a right turn leads to Lake Jean, the park office, and picnic facilities).

After three smaller waterfalls, reach the top of Ganoga Falls. From a narrow ledge, there is a spectacular and scary view to the bottom of the cascade 94 feet below. A series of switchbacks leads down alongside the falls. A short fence protects you from slipping off the edge for the first 20 feet. At the bottom, a slippery side path leads down to the pool at the base of the falls. Continue on the main trail past six more falls, each one unique. You again reach Waters Meet at 5 miles. Continue straight ahead and retrace your steps along Kitchen Creek and back to your car at 6.8 miles.

There have been recent improvements to this scenic national landmark, to accommodate the many visitors. New trail signs, benches, retainers of natural materials, and stone steps cut into the shale are designed to preserve the natural beauty of the area. Because of the many accidents that have occurred, the park service may add railings at some steeper sections of the trail. The best, least-crowded time to visit is on a weekday in the spring or fall.

There is additional hiking in Ricketts Glen State Park, including the 13-mile Cherry Run Loop Trail and the 5-mile Ganoga Loop Trail. Stop at the park office off PA 118 near Lake Jean for a trail map.

PART FOUR

NORTH WOODS

Sullivan, Susquehanna, Bradford, Wyoming, Lycoming, and Montour Counties

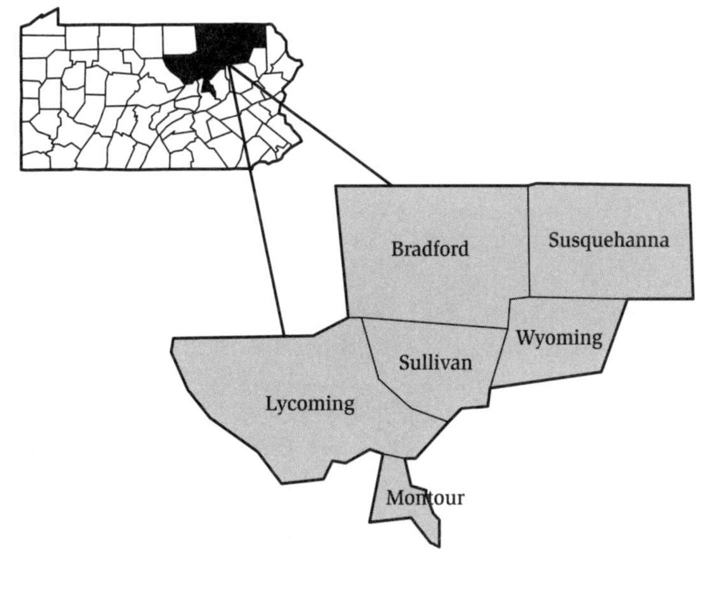

34. GREAT BEND

Distance	6 miles
Elevation	1,100 feet
Time to hike	3 hours
Surface	Grassy woods road (may be muddy)
Interesting features	Many opportunities to see wildlife, mountain views
Facilities	None
Hunting	Yes

Directions

From I-81 (Exit 68) near the New York line:

1. North on PA 171 for .1 mile to traffic light (US 11).
2. Turn left (south) onto US 11 (cross Susquehanna River) for .2 mile to Harmony Road
3. Turn left onto Harmony Road (SR 1010) for 2.4 miles to Smokie Hollow Road
4. Turn right onto Smokie Hollow Road (TR 698) (watch for game-lands sign)
5. Drive 1 mile to parking area on the left

Coordinates 41°56'45"N; 75°42'19"W

This remote hike in State Game Lands 35 is located near Great Bend, a curving meander carved by the north branch of the Susquehanna River through sandstone and shale bedrock. We found considerable evidence of wildlife but no other humans in this isolated corner of the state. If you walk quietly, you are bound to see the animals. In the fall during deer season, however, limit hiking to Sundays, when hunting is not allowed in Pennsylvania. If you hike here in mosquito and tick season, from spring to early fall, we suggest a long-sleeved shirt, long pants, and insect repellent.

Begin by walking uphill (south) on the dirt access road. The woods are composed of mixed hardwoods, with blackberries along the road. At .4 mile, notice Little Egypt Creek to the right in a hemlock grove. The dirt road can be muddy after a rain, providing a perfect opportunity to see wildlife tracks. We saw bear scat and a footprint 6 inches wide. Male black bears can weigh up to 700 pounds, and we were glad not to encounter the owner of that foot.

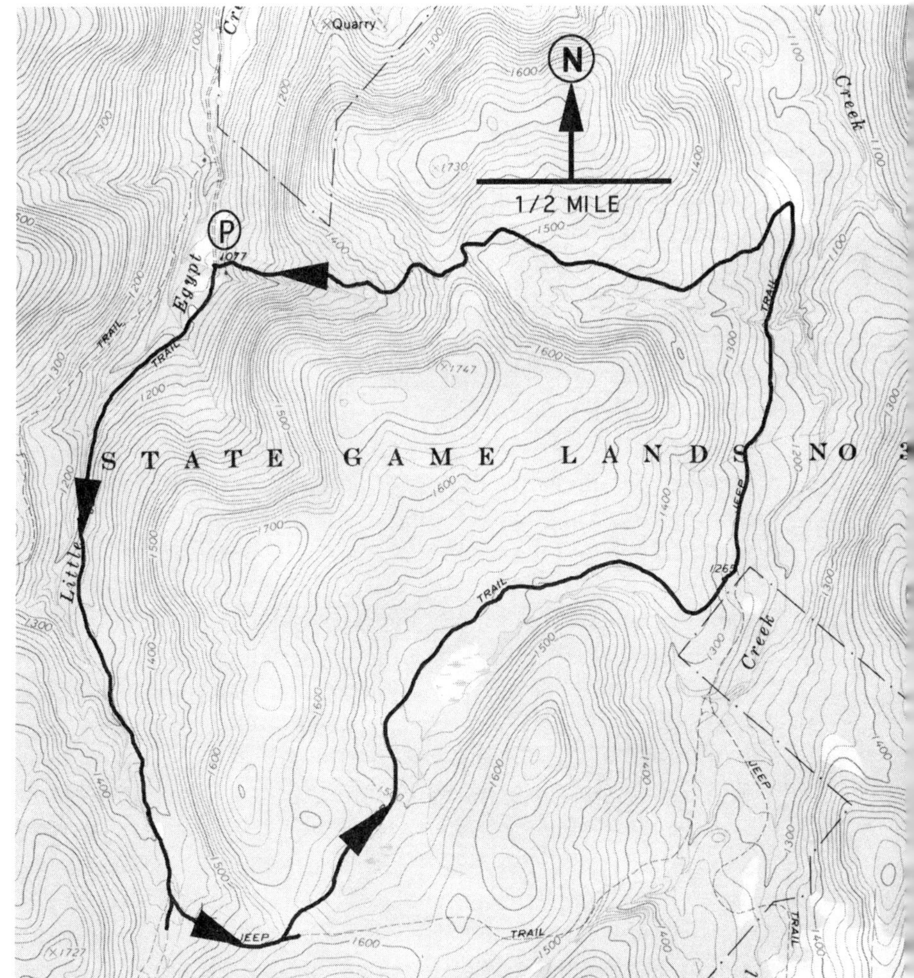

As you continue uphill, note a small pond to the left at 1.2 miles, then another one on the right, followed by a fairly large swamp. The swamp is habitat for a variety of waterfowl and wading birds and continues on the right for the next .5 mile.

When you reach a parking area, look for a metal gate to your left and a tree with three blue strips. Turn left (southwest), walking around the gate, on a grassy track closed to traffic. In 50 feet, another road comes in from the right. Continue straight ahead uphill, over a grassy 20-foot-wide mown path.

At 2.1 miles, bear left (north) at a Y intersection of woods roads, continuing to follow blue blazes. The trail becomes more level and then slopes downhill for 2 easy miles through second-growth woods. You step over numerous tiny streams and rivulets that feed a swamp on the right. Many animal tracks can be seen in the mud, and salamanders, tadpoles, and tiny frogs live in the puddles. We also found some large clumps of turkey feathers—evidence perhaps of a fatal encounter with a fox or other predator.

Reach a T intersection in a hemlock grove; turn left, heading north. At 4.2 miles, cross Mitchell Creek over a culvert. A 30-foot-high cascade waterfall tumbles over the rock layers. Notice the layered shale outcroppings along the stream.

At 4.6 miles, the woods open up to a meadow with lovely views of Smokey Mountain to the north and Maunatome Mountain to the northwest. The Susquehanna River in the valley below flows south into Pennsylvania, then turns north again into New York State. You cannot see the river because of the thick vegetation. Continue through an abandoned field and an old apple orchard. Just after a large apple tree, turn left uphill on a woods road. Here a deer jumped in front of us and darted up the road before reentering the woods. Berry-covered branches stacked by the road by the Game Commission provide food and cover for pheasants, quail, turkeys, and grouse. If you flush any game birds, you will probably hear the beating of their wings before you see them.

Continue for another mile; after a long uphill climb, reach a road intersection. Continue straight ahead (west) on an old woods road. Some of the trees are blue-blazed. From here, the road goes steeply downhill through mixed hardwoods. Continue straight ahead to a metal gate and your car at 6 miles.

35. SALT SPRINGS STATE PARK

Distance	2 miles
Elevation	190 feet
Time to hike	1 hour
Surface	Rocky trail (you may get your feet wet in the stream)
Interesting features	Three waterfalls, virgin hemlocks, an unusual salt spring, and a fascinating legend
Facilities	Rest rooms, picnic tables; no fresh water
Hunting	Yes

Directions

From I-81 (Exit 67) near the New York line:

1. West on PA 492 for .6 mile to stop sign (end of PA 492)
2. Turn left (south) on US 11 for 1 mile to PA 706
3. Turn right (west) on PA 706 for 7.1 miles to PA 29
4. Turn right (north) on PA 29 for 5.7 miles to SR 4008 (just after crossing Silver Creek in Franklin Forks)
5. Turn left on SR 4008 and drive .9 mile to park entrance
6. Turn left into park entrance; continue .1 mile down a dirt road crossing Silver Creek to the parking lot

Coordinates 41°54'49"N; 75°51'57"W

Salt Springs State Park includes three lovely cascade waterfalls, a salt spring, and a legend. In the early nineteenth century, a settler named Robert Rosbach was ambushed and wounded at his nearby farm by hostile Indians. His wife, Emmeline, and children escaped. Robert was taken captive, and Emmeline followed the party from a distance. The Indians took him to Fall Creek and made camp between the first and second waterfalls. An owl, startled by the smoke from the campfire, shrieked and gave away their location to a war party of Oneida Indians. The Oneida attacked from the ridge above. As the battle moved away from the ravine, Rosbach was left tied to a tree. Emmeline found and freed her husband. Believing in the healing powers of the nearby salt spring, Emmeline led him there and bathed his wounds. Unfortunately, Robert died anyway, and his grieving widow sadly concealed his body in the rocks.

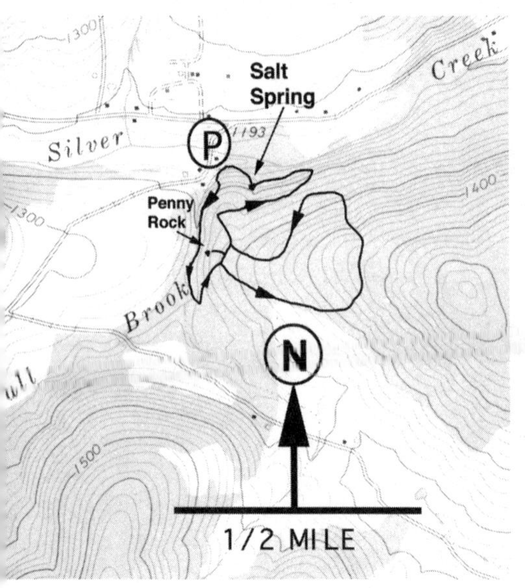

Returning to her friends, she bade them to "seek the remains of my love beneath the shadow of the precipice of the salt spring." This short and scenic hike leads you past the waterfalls, the precipice, and the salt spring.

At the parking lot, cross a small wooden footbridge over Fall Brook to a large trail sign. The Fall Brook Trail is well marked with red painted markers tacked to trees and red blazes on the rocks. You walk along—and sometimes in—Fall Brook, among giant virgin hemlocks up to 11 feet in circumference. Hemlocks in this area, and the tannin in their bark, were once used in the leather tanning industry. These trees along Fall Brook were too remote to harvest and grew to majestic heights. At .2 mile, you reach the first waterfall. Depending on recent rainfall, you may actually walk in the streambed. It is a tricky climb up the falls, using toeholds in the rock and grasping tree roots for support. During spring runoff, you may need to leave the streambed and climb the very steep hemlock-strewn slope to the top of the ridge. At .3 mile and .5 mile, you come to the second and third cascade waterfalls, cut into the rock layers. Climb out of the gorge, following the red arrows on the rocks where two streams converge. At the top of the ridge at .6 mile, turn left, following the Fall Brook Trail. The deep hemlock gorge and creek are on your left; ferns, ironwoods, and other hardwoods are on your right.

At 1 mile, you reach an intersection with the orange-blazed Woodland Trail and the blue-blazed Penny Rock Trail. Turn right on the Woodland Trail Loop, following small orange wooden arrows and markers tacked to the trees. You return to the Fall Brook Trail at 1.5 miles. Turn left 100 feet to the Penny Rock Trail.

It is a .2-mile round-trip to Penny Rock. Emmeline no doubt concealed Robert's body below this rock, just as the legend describes, "beneath the shadow of the precipice of the salt spring." It is certainly a serene resting place, overlooking the hemlock-filled gorge far below. Visitors have left pennies, nickels, and dimes for good luck on the large, flat rock.

Return to the Fall Brook Trail and turn left. At 1.8 miles, pass the Hemlock Trail coming in from the left, which leads back to Penny Rock. Descend from the ridge to the Salt Spring at 1.9 miles.

Aboriginal Indians believed in the magical properties of the spring, and it was a closely guarded source of salt long before settlers arrived. In 1813, there were commercial efforts to mine the salt; eventually the Susquehanna Salt Works Company sank a 650-foot well, and a total of 20 tons of high-quality dairy salt were extracted. By 1871, the mine was abandoned as no longer profitable. Don't try to drink from the spring. The water contains sulfur and iron as well as salt and has a decidedly "rotten-egg" smell.

Walk through a quiet picnic grove and return to your car at 2 miles.

36. JOE GMITER TRAIL

Distance	8.2 miles
Elevation	1,690 feet
Time to hike	6 hours
Surface	Rough trail, woods road
Interesting features	Steep climbs, mountain views (in winter and spring)
Facilities	None
Hunting	Yes

Directions

From US 11 in Wilkes-Barre:

1. North on PA 309 for 5.8 miles to PA 415
2. PA 309 veers right; continue straight ahead (north) on PA 415 for 9.5 miles to PA 29
3. Straight ahead (north) on PA 29 for 3 miles to Market Street in Noxen
4. Straight ahead on Market Street (PA 29 turns right)
5. Cross bridge over Bowman Creek; at .1 mile, turn left onto School Street (SR 3002) for 2.2 miles
6. Turn left at Sorber Mountain Road (crossing a one-lane bridge over Bowman Creek) for 1 mile to parking area on the left

Coordinates 41°24'01"N; 76°05'24"W

You should be in top condition and wear your hiking boots for this rugged hike in State Game Lands 57, the second-largest in Pennsylvania. The trail takes you up one side of Sorber Mountain, down the other side, and then up and over again. You will be climbing a total of 1,690 feet, and there are several climbs of 300 feet in just a quarter of a mile. The trail system was built by the Susquehanna Trailers Hiking Club and named for Joe Gmiter, who was president of the club for many years.

The trail is not well maintained, and your usual hiking pace may be slowed by numerous blowdowns and small stream crossings, as well as steep climbs. However, the trail follows the well-marked game-lands boundary, and there is little chance of getting lost.

At the parking lot, there is a large sign showing the trail system. Red, yellow, blue, and orange markers blaze trails of 3.25 to 10.5

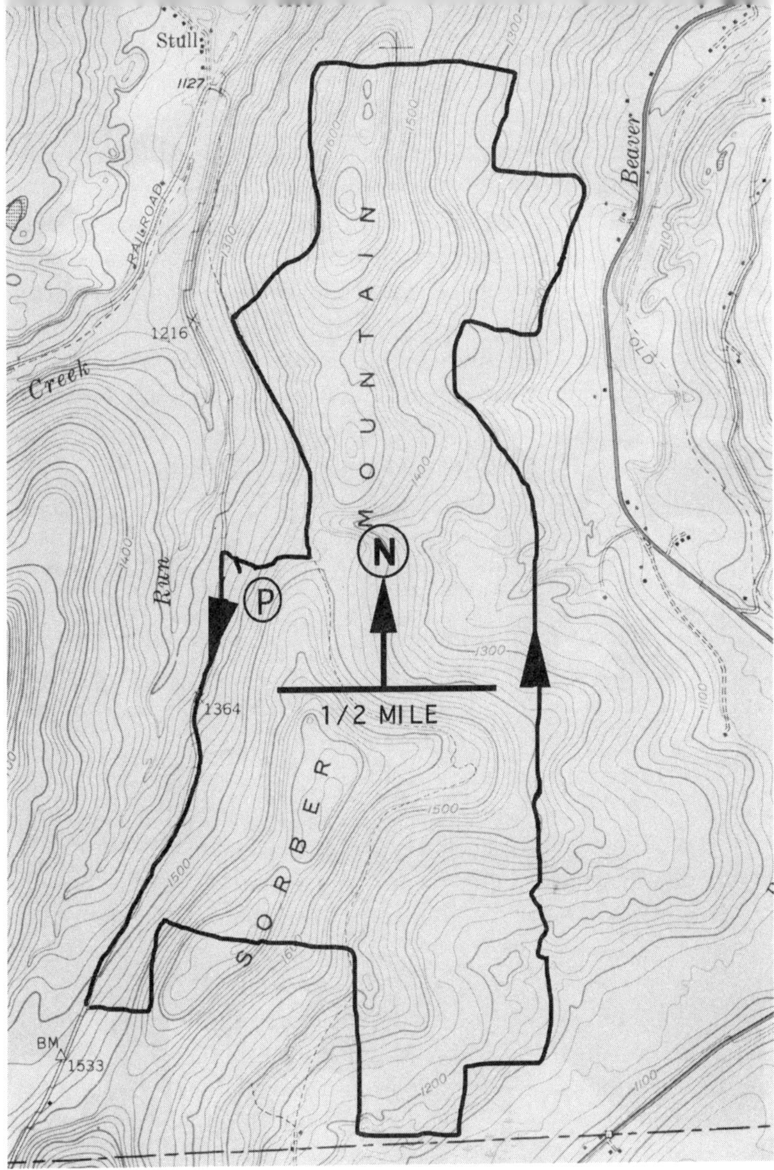

miles in length; however, these mileages are overestimated. You will be following the longest, the orange trail, which is actually 8.2 miles.

Begin hiking southwest on the dirt road you drove in on. Colored metal discs tacked to trees indicate the trail route. Hike in a counterclockwise direction; there are only a few blazes to mark the trail if hiked clockwise. At 1 mile, turn left (north) at the edge of a field along a stone row, following the orange and blue discs.

The game-lands boundary is blazed white by the Game Commission. Boundary corners are prominently marked by pipes set in stones and painted white with identifying numbers. Property owners on your right have blazed the trees yellow. Some trees painted white and yellow appear to be claimed by both the state and private owners.

Follow the line of disputed boundary trees to the narrow ridge at the top of Sorber Mountain at 1.5 miles. A distinct line separates thick stands of mountain laurel and huckleberries at the top. There are nice views to the southeast in the spring and winter only.

Continue downhill, crossing a woods road at 2 miles. You soon reach several farm ponds and a fence bordering a field. The trail turns north, crossing several small streams that feed a swamp on your right.

Notice the No Trespassing signs on property owned by the H. L. Pistol and Rifle Club of Noxen. There were at least four deer blinds on the hike route. Although we noted many deer signs, the animals, understandably wary of humans, stayed out of sight.

The trail continues up and down several ravines, with more stream crossings. At 6 miles, just after a junkyard on private property, you reach the lowest point of the hike. A swamp on your right, fed by Beaver Creek, is maintained by a beaver family. The beavers have taken down many medium-sized trees, some too large for them to move. You may see their lodge in the swamp. Turn left here, along an old stone row.

A cool stand of hemlocks and a fresh breeze reward you for the steep climb to the top of Sorber Mountain at 6.7 miles. The trail goes sharply downhill, then slopes up again through thick mountain laurel. After another downhill, pass a trail register at 7.3 miles adjacent to a logging road. Two wrecked vehicles were apparently dragged in and abandoned on the logging road. You soon reach an old woods road; turn left. Many of the medium to large trees on the right have been marked yellow for harvesting.

At 8 miles, turn right at an intersection with the red and blue trails, then go downhill to your car.

37. EAGLES MERE

Distance	4 miles
Elevation	340 feet
Time to hike	1¾ hours
Surface	Railroad grade, rocky woods trail
Interesting features	Historic town of Eagles Mere, mountain laurel (the state plant) blooming in May and June
Facilities	At Conservancy Cabin
Hunting	No

Directions

From US 6 at Towanda:

1. South on connector road (SR 2027, Main Street) for 1.9 miles to US 220
2. Turn left (south) on US 220 for 26.2 miles to PA 42 at Laporte
3. Turn right (south) on PA 42 for 5.4 miles
4. Turn right at the sign "Eagles Mere" (at the outlet pond)
5. Continue for .1 mile; park in front of the outlet pond

Coordinates 41°24'39"N; 76°34'26"W

At the turn of the century, Eagles Mere was a thriving resort with many stately homes and three elegant hotels. Located at the crossroads of the logging and tanning industries in Sullivan County, it was served by the Susquehanna and Eagles Mere Railroad from 1906 to 1922. As these industries declined, the town fell on hard economic times. In 1980, a group of concerned home owners banded together to purchase the last hotel, the Crestmont Inn, to save it from commercial development. This effort led to the Eagles Mere Conservancy. The conservancy owns 250 acres of wooded mountain slopes to the east of Eagles Mere Lake. Three miles of blazed conservancy trails connect with other trails laid out over a hundred years ago with a historic railroad grade. The conservancy also holds easements over private lands. Today, Eagles Mere is still popular as an upscale summer residence, and the town supports many quaint and exclusive shops, art festivals, and the like.

Just ahead is the Outlet Pond, 50 percent covered with water lilies, which bloom in May and June. Walk up the road. Just to your

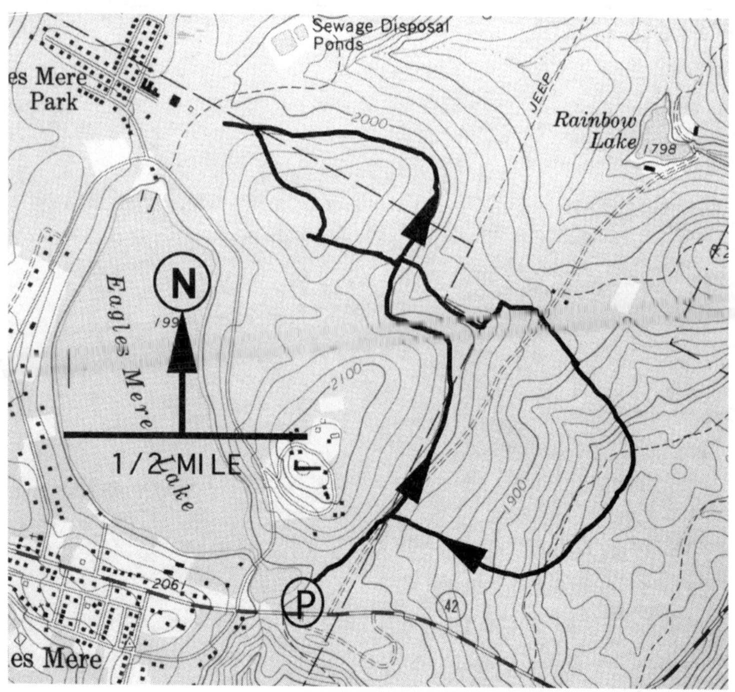

right is the Conservancy Cabin, circa 1734, which serves as an education center. You can pick up a map of the trail system here.

Continue ahead on the old railroad grade through mixed hardwoods. The Buff B Trail, your return route, comes in from the right; stay on the railroad grade. Just beyond a row of spruces, a private road parallels the grade a short distance. At 1 mile, you reach a Y intersection. Bear right on the level, more traveled grade. Mineral Springs Avenue, a gravel road closed to traffic, joins the trail at 1.3 miles.

At a wooden gate at 1.5 miles, at Eagles Mere Park, turn left on the red-blazed Red Arrow Path. Shortly, pass a sign and path to Big Spring and Beach. At 1.9 miles, the peach-blazed Buff B Trail comes in from the left. Continue ahead a few hundred feet to Eagle Rocks, a layered rock outcropping. Backtrack, then follow the Buff B Trail downhill on a rocky, mossy trail through mixed hardwoods. Cross the railroad grade. Walk along a private property line adjacent to an

8-foot-high wire deer fence. Cross a private road, staying on the Buff B Trail. The trail continues in a long loop, intersecting the Buff C Trail twice, crosses the private road, and returns to the railroad grade at 3.9 miles. Turn left and return to your car at 4 miles.

Other trails in the area are worth exploring. The Loyalsock Trail connects with the north end of the Red Arrow Path. The Laurel Path (2 miles long), circling Eagles Mere Lake, dates from 1895. Mountain laurel and sheep laurel, up to 20 feet high, can be found all along the path and are covered with pale pink and white blossoms in May and June.

For information, contact Eagles Mere Conservancy, Inc., Eagles Mere, PA 17731.

38. WORLDS END STATE PARK

Distance	3.5 miles
Elevation	1,000 feet
Time to hike	2 hours 20 minutes
Surface	Rocky trail
Interesting features	Loyalsock Trail, views
Facilities	Picnic tables, rest rooms at top of Canyon Vista and campground
Hunting	Yes

Directions

From US 6 at Towanda:

1. South on connector road (SR 2027, Main Street) for 1.9 miles to US 220
2. Turn left (south) on US 220 for 25.8 miles to PA 154
3. Turn right (north) on PA 154 for 6.4 miles
4. Turn left and bear left again into parking lot just past the camp office (if that lot is full, continue ahead to a second lot in the campground)

Coordinates 41°28'09"N; 76°34'17"W (41°28'01"N; 76°34'07"W for the second parking lot)

Worlds End State Park is located in a narrow S-shaped valley of the Loyalsock Creek in the heart of the Endless Mountains. The park was called "Whirls End" at one time, a reference to the swirling S-curve of the creek, once an obstacle to logs floated down the river by the Central Pennsylvania Lumber Company. The land was acquired from the lumber company in the early 1930s and renamed Worlds End State Park in 1943.

Walk up the road around the camp office to the Canyon Vista Trail, blazed with blue metal diamonds tacked to trees. The trail ascends steeply until .5 mile, where the main Loyalsock Trail crosses it. Continue straight ahead on the Canyon Vista Trail, which soon levels to a plateau on the west side of the mountain. The trail winds through mixed hardwoods, hemlocks, and mountain laurel, with fine views to Double Run Gorge on the right. At .8 mile, turn sharply left (northeast) on the combined Loyalsock Link and Canyon Vista Trails. The trail again ascends steeply.

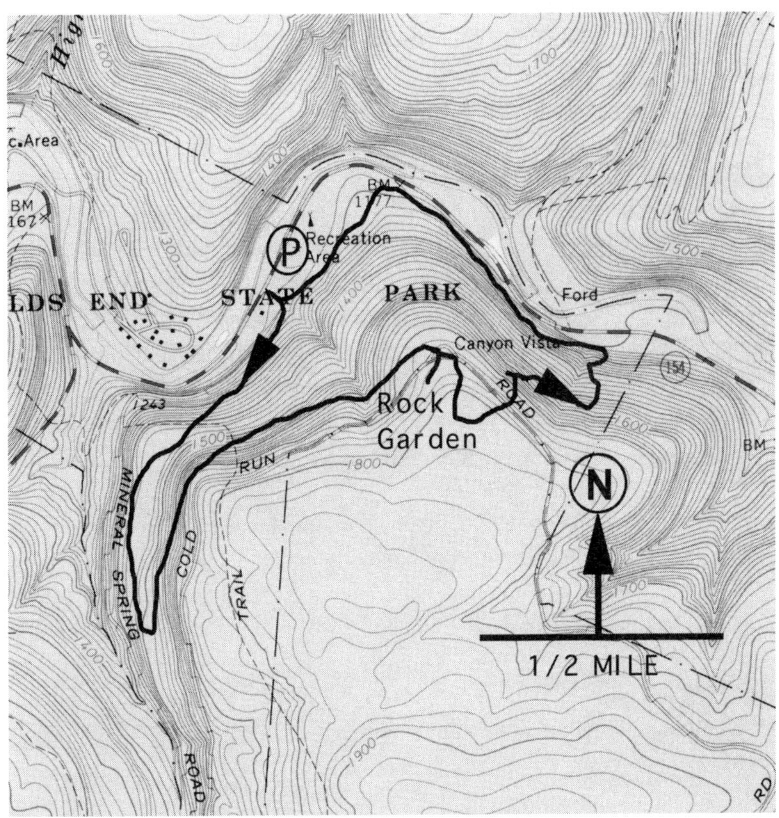

Your climb is rewarded at 1.6 miles by spectacular views of the Loyalsock Creek valley in a hemlock grove at Canyon Vista. Notice how the horizon seems relatively flat. The mountains ahead are really a plateau composed of resistant shale and sandstone. Softer sedimentary layers have been carved by streams into deep ravines. A wooden fence protects careless hikers from falling off into space. At the edge of the parking lot, there is a sign for the "Rock Garden." A .2-mile round-trip leads farther uphill past outhouses to a collection of jumbled conglomerate and sandstone boulders as big as cabins.

Turn east on the road, and just past the parking lot pick up the main Loyalsock Trail, lined with blackberries. The Link Trail turns right at 1.7 miles; you continue ahead on the Loyalsock Trail. At 1.9 miles, cross Cold Stream Road. As you head downhill, watch closely for the blue blazes of the Canyon Vista Trail and turn right, uphill, at 2 miles.

The Canyon Vista Trail in this section is well blazed, but blowdowns frequently obstruct the trail. At the top of a rise, there is another jumbled collection of huge stone blocks. Crevasses, caves, rocky ledges, and overhangs create a labyrinth. Shortly, the trail heads steeply down the mountain on a series of switchbacks. We passed a patch of cardinal flowers, with brilliant scarlet blooms, in late summer. These showy, attractive flowers are scarce due to overpicking. Black raspberries and thistles also abound in sunny areas.

The trail descends and runs parallel to PA 154, reaching the campground at 3 miles. Still on the blue-blazed trail, turn left and follow the camp road to reach your car at 3.5 miles.

39. CHILISUAGI TRAIL

Distance	5.2 miles
Elevation	320 feet
Time to hike	2 hours
Surface	Gravel, crushed stone, and mown path through meadow and woodland
Interesting features	Water- and shorebirds, fossils, field and woodland habitats, 165-acre lake, fine nature exhibits at new Visitors Center
Facilities	Benches along trail; picnic tables, grills, rest rooms, water at picnic areas; no pets or bicycles allowed
Hunting	No

Directions

From I-80 (Exit 33) north of Bloomsburg:

1. West on PA 54 for 4.3 miles
2. Turn right (east) on PA 254 (Washingtonville Road) for .5 mile
3. Turn left on SR 1003 (Pennsylvania Power and Light Road) for 3.5 miles
4. Turn right on SR 1006 for .4 mile
5. Turn left into Montour Preserve; pick up a map at the Visitors Center and continue for .3 mile to the Goose Cove Overlook parking lot (birders should request a pass to the Goose Cove Wildlife Refuge at the Visitors Center)

Coordinates 41°06'08"N; 76°39'54"W

Every spring and fall, incoming flights of ducks and geese appear at regular intervals on the horizon, swoop in over Lake Chillisquaque dam, and touch down on the water. Constructed in the late 1960s, the lake has become a favorite stopping-off place for loons, grebes, ducks, geese, and mergansers. The name is derived from Chillisquaque Creek; *Chillisquaque* is an Iroquois word meaning "song of the wild goose," an especially apt name. Migrating warblers, hawks, and eagles are also regular visitors.

At the Goose Cove Overlook, you find the first of eighteen interpretive signs along the trail. From the parking lot, continue walking up the road past a white pine plantation on your left to a picnic area. The Chilisuagi Trail starts at the north end of the grassy field on

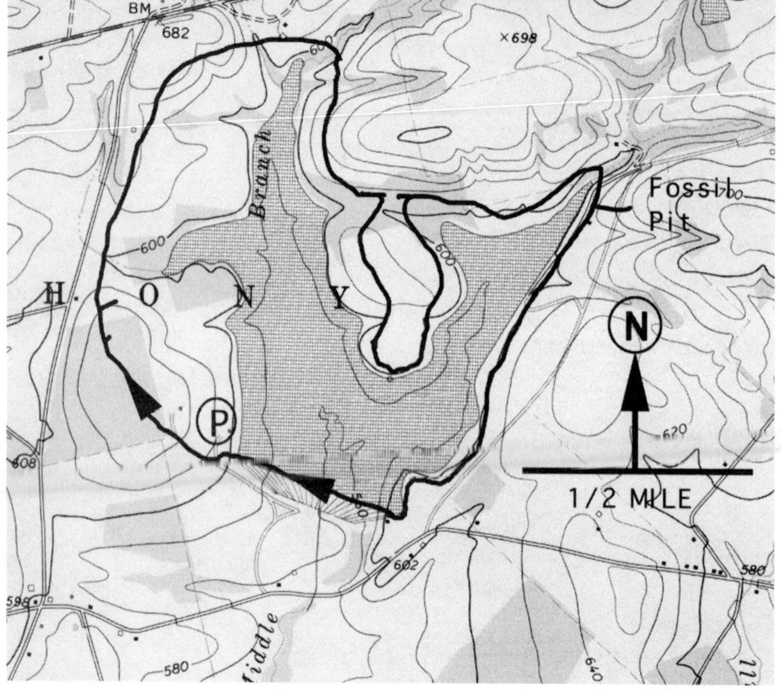

a wide mown path through a wildflower-filled meadow. A wildlife refuge on your right continues for the next mile; the Oak Woods and Alder Swamp Trails enter the refuge and end at bird blinds overlooking the Goose Cove inlet. (A permit to enter the refuge is required and available at the Visitors Center.)

The trail surface is gravel through alternating fields, fencerows, and forest of large oaks, black walnuts, hickories, and tulip poplars. At .6 mile, the trail parallels the PPL Road for a short distance. Overlooks provide views into the 146-acre refuge and the lake; benches invite a rest along the trail. Meadows are gradually reverting to woodlands. At 1.1 miles, you reach foundation remains of an old farmstead. The trail continues along fencerows and the edges of fields in agricultural areas of the preserve.

Cross the middle branch of Chillisquaque Creek, the main lake inlet, on a wooden bridge, continuing through meadow reverting to woodland. Pass larches and a pine plantation, then enter the Hickory Hollow Woods, which was logged over perhaps thirty years ago. Old stumps and tree trunks are scattered among the second-growth trees.

At 1.8 miles, you reach the start of the .75-mile Ridgefield Point Trail, through fields reverting to forest and stands of pine and larch. As you approach the lake, intersecting mown paths cross the trail.

Simply keep to the right along the lake, where you have a fine view to Goose Cove inlet and swamp, with skeletons of alders. Here we saw a blue-winged teal with a single duckling in the grasses beside the trail. She allowed us to approach to within 10 feet before leading her youngster into the lake.

The trail rejoins the Chilisuagi Trail and continues to Jellyfish Cove. Cattails and rushes along the lake edge are favorite nesting areas for waterfowl. Tree sparrows, tufted titmice, chickadees, mockingbirds, and wrens, among others, find food and cover in the shrubs.

Cross another well-built wooden bridge and turn right. At a sign for the Bluebird Trail, turn left to walk up to a parking lot, where you can pick up a guide to that trail. Cross the paved road, walk around a yellow metal gate, and follow the gravel road to the fossil pit. Collecting is permitted. Look for fossils of trilobites and crinoids in newly exposed shale.

Return to the Chilisuagi Trail, which runs for a short distance with the .75-mile Bluebird Trail. If you like, continue on the trail through a meadow containing nesting boxes and attractive habitat for eastern bluebirds.

The Chilisuagi Trail closely follows the lake. The crushed stone path is elevated over marshy areas. Alders, hawthorns, dogwoods, autumn olives, currants, and multiflora roses provide food and cover for songbirds.

Reach the Heron Cove picnic area. Here you find a large variety of ducks, geese, and loons; some are quite tame. You are requested not to feed them. Cross a parking lot; the Sunset Point Overlook is on a bluff to your left. As you approach the dam, twin smokestacks and cooling towers of the power plant lie ahead, about 3 miles away. The lake was built to provide emergency cooling water to the Pennsylvania Power and Light coal-fired electric-generating plant. Turn right, walk around a metal gate, and cross the dam, where you have a fine view of the entire lake. Complete the loop at the Goose Cove Overlook.

There have been recent improvements and expansion of the fine Visitors Center, which contains educational exhibits, hands-on activities for children, and an outdoor wildlife feeding area. Contact the park at PP&L Montour Preserve, RR 1 Box 292, Turbotville, PA 17772, or at www.papl.com/community/landmgmt.htm.

40. MOUNT PISGAH

Distance	6.8 miles
Elevation	1,180 feet
Time to hike	4 hours
Surface	Rocky woods road, mown path through meadows
Interesting features	Views from summit of Mount Pisgah; paper birch forest; wildlife—turkeys, deer, bears; Stephen Foster Lake
Facilities	Rest rooms, water at trailhead parking lot; occasional benches along trail; picnic tables, rest rooms at summit of Mount Pisgah
Hunting	Yes

Directions

From US 6 in Towanda:

1. West on US 6 for 10.8 miles to SR 3019 in West Burlington
2. Turn right on SR 3019 (at Krauss store on right) for 2.4 miles to SR 4015
3. Turn right on SR 4015 (at a T intersection) for .5 mile
4. Park at the parking lot on the right side by the lake (the park office is .6 mile farther on the right side)

Coordinates 41°01'07"N; 76°25'40"W

During the late 1800s, a resort hotel complete with observation tower was built atop Mount Pisgah to accommodate well-to-do summer visitors from the cities of the Northeast, who came to enjoy the spring water, clean air, and scenic views. There are no signs left of the hotel, but Mount Pisgah is still a great place to visit at any time of the year. Most of the hike is within Mount Pisgah State Park; the summit is within the county park.

The Oh! Susanna Trail (remember the song?) circles Stephen Foster (the composer) Lake for an easy 2 miles. We suggest a more challenging hike on the Ridge Trail to the summit of Mount Pisgah.

The trail begins across from the parking lot on the Mill Stream Nature Trail (to your left is the return route). Walk alongside the lake and adjacent marshland through dense hemlocks. Look for signs of beavers in the wetlands on your right—lodges, channels in

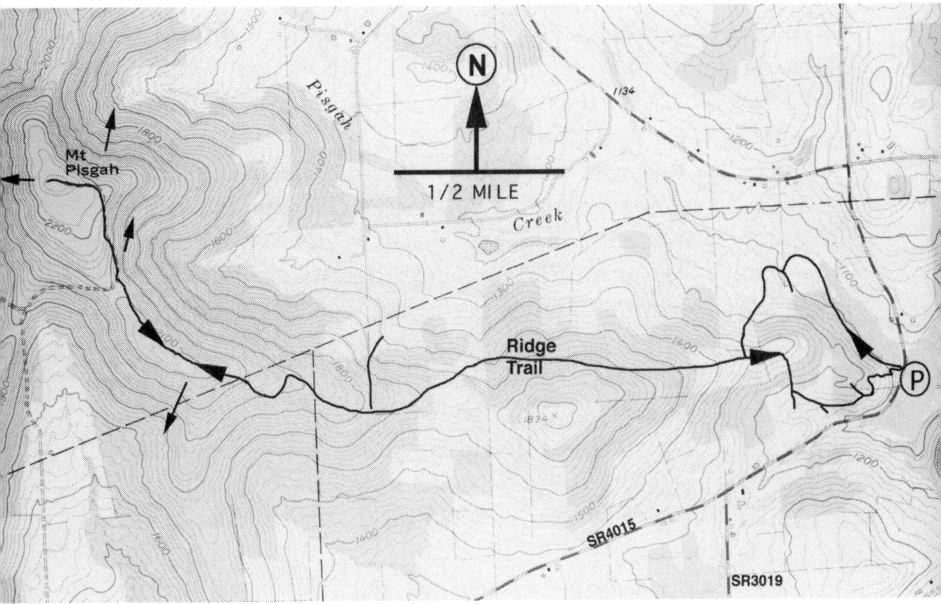

the marsh, cut saplings. Moist areas in the path support a variety of colorful mushrooms and toadstools.

Turn right at an intersection with the Pine Tree Trail at .6 mile. Old stone and tree-stump fences provide evidence of early attempts to farm the rocky soil. The hemlocks give way to a second-growth forest of maple, beech, and birch. The trail gradually steepens, with more tree varieties; some are recognizable by their distinctive bark, such as shagbark hickory. Striped maple (moosewood) is a small to medium tree with a large, flat leaf. Its bark is an unusual striped green. Paper birch is also easily recognized by its bark.

At .8 mile, bear right on the Ridge Trail. Paper birch predominates here. These trees do not grow very large, and their open foliage allows the distinctive bark to be appreciated even in the summer. In the winter, you have a view of valley farmland to the north and south. The Ridge Trail takes you through the most isolated areas of the park. A hike in the winter as late as March reveals deer, raccoon, black bear, and bobcat tracks in the snow. The trail is steep in places, ascending over 1,000 feet in a little over 2 miles. Fortunately, there are strategically located benches so you can catch your breath before several of the steeper climbs.

Just after a hemlock grove, you reach two trail signs. One indicates the county park 1.2 miles ahead; the other sign indicates the Hicks Hollow Trail to the right, a .7-mile descent to a dirt road. Continue straight ahead on the Ridge Trail.

Just after the signs, the trail levels to a plateau. In spring and summer, an abandoned farm field ahead is filled with wildflowers. In early July, milkweed, black-eyed Susan, goldenrod, and clover are in bloom, visited by a variety of butterflies. Your objective, Mount Pisgah, is straight ahead to the northwest, topped with a microwave tower.

After crossing the meadow, head uphill on a rocky woods road. When we were there, a flock of sixty to seventy crows began crowing and circling noisily—a defensive strategy called "mobbing." If one crow sees a predator—a hawk, for example—it gives an assembly call. Every crow within earshot quickly flies to the source and attacks the predator.

Soon the woods begin to thin out. In July, look for red raspberries on both sides of the trail. At 2.4 miles, walk past a metal gate to enter the county park. After 500 feet, you come to a picnic table and somewhat obscured views to the southwest of Bradford County farmland. Continue straight ahead on the woods road through county parkland to an asphalt road. Turn right uphill to an overlook to the north; then walk past picnic tables and camp facilities to the microwave tower.

There is a legend that 200 years ago, an Oneida Indian chief known as Wetonah would climb this mountain to meditate and enjoy the views. The Oneida once owned over 6 million acres of land to the north and west of here. Chief Wetonah's remains were buried at the summit of Mount Pisgah, and it is said that his spirit remains here still. Walk around the microwave tower for overlooks of the Endless Mountains to the west and northeast, the ancestral land of the Oneida.

Return down the asphalt road to the Ridge Trail to retrace your steps. This time, pass the Pine Tree Trail and stay on the Ridge Trail to a meadow. Turn left onto the Snowmobile Trail to return to your car at 6.8 miles.

41. LOYALSOCK TRAIL

Distance	7.2 miles
Elevation	1,400 feet
Time to hike	4 hours
Surface	Rocky woods trail, abandoned railroad grades and logging roads
Interesting features	Angel Falls, vista to Kettle Creek Gorge Natural Area, historic Loyalsock Trail
Facilities	None
Hunting	Yes

Directions

From US 6 at Towanda:

1. South on connector road (SR 2027, Main Street) for 1.9 miles to US 220
2. Turn left (south) on US 220 for 26.2 miles to PA 42 at Laporte
3. Turn right (south) on PA 42 for 9.3 miles to Brunnerdale Road
4. Turn right on Brunnerdale Road for 4 miles to parking lot on the right

Coordinates 41°23'15"N; 76°40'11"W

This rugged hike on the Loyalsock Trail (LT) in Wyoming State Forest visits a beautiful waterfall and natural area. Bobcats, coyotes, red and gray foxes, and bears are regularly spotted here. The 59-mile LT, first established in 1953, is one of the oldest in Pennsylvania. It takes advantage of long-abandoned timber roads and railroad grades, reminders of the logging industry, which was vital to the economy of the region in the early part of the century. The LT is marked with metal discs (can lids) painted yellow with the red letters LT. It is also blazed yellow with a red horizontal bar. Turns are marked with double blazes or a yellow arrow. Two side trips, to Angel Falls and the Kettle Creek Vista, are included in the mileage and hiking time.

Pick up the LT at the edge of the parking lot as it follows Ogdonia Creek. Shortly cross Brunnerdale Run, a small tributary. The LT continues along the stream, then turns sharply right, ascending on an old woods road at .4 mile. The trail turns left on another woods

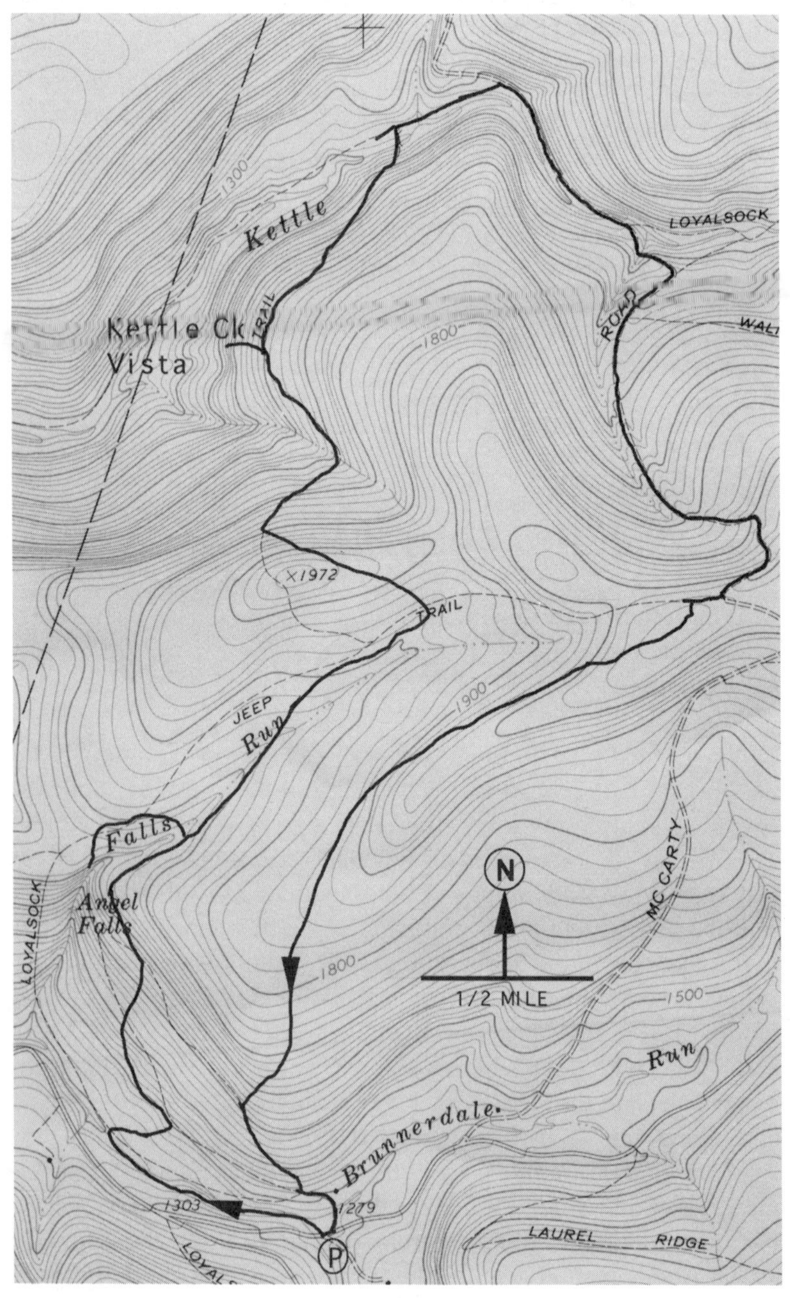
1300
Kettle
TRAIL
Kettle Ck
Vista
1800
LOYALSOCK
ROAD
WAL
X1972
TRAIL
1900
JEEP
Run
Falls
Angel
Falls
LOYALSOCK
N
MC CARTY
1800
1/2 MILE
1500
Run
Brunnerdale
1303
1279
P
LAUREL
RIDGE

road; then at .7 mile, it turns right on a trail. Turn left on a second woods road, then right again on an old skid trail that climbs steeply uphill 130 feet.

The trail levels off somewhat until you reach the side trail to Angel Falls at 1.2 miles. It is a .6-mile round-trip to the falls. The LT used to go to the falls but was rerouted by the Forest Service because of overuse and erosion. The area around the falls has been closed to rock climbing, rappelling, and camping, and seeded areas are protected by an orange fence. However, hiking on the trail to the top, then down to the base of the falls, is permitted. The amount of water that falls over the 180-foot rock face varies with the season; in midsummer, the flow resembles that from a garden hose. Angel Falls is the highest falls on the LT and is said to be named for the highest waterfall in the world, Angel Falls in Venezuela. There are two more falls downstream.

Returning to the trail, the LT passes through an expanse of club mosses and ground pines and then crosses Falls Run. The LT crosses a grassy jeep trail at 2.6 miles.

For this hike, stay on the LT as it ascends steeply between large boulders to a level, grassy plateau. The trail then descends around the ridge, losing 400 feet in .5 mile. As the trail levels at 3.2 miles, a short (.1-mile) blue-blazed side trail leads to the edge of a rock outcropping. From high on a rocky overlook, you have a fine view of the Kettle Creek Natural Area. We spotted a scarlet tanager. He allowed us to approach fairly closely and was quite noticeable in the dark woods, brilliant scarlet with black wings and tail.

Returning to the LT, the trail continues a descent around the ridge to Kettle Creek. Cross Kettle Creek and walk upstream on an old railroad grade. This narrow-gauge track of the Susquehanna and Eagles Mere Railroad operated from 1906 to 1922; it brought tourists to the Eagles Mere resort and moved timber to the sawmill village of Sonesville. At 4.4 miles, the LT turns left (north). Continue ahead, ignoring Ryans Trail on your left. Stay on the old grade (now McCarty Road) as it fords Kettle Creek and continues uphill. McCarty Road was named for Sumner McCarty, the first forest ranger in this area (1930–50). At 4.6 miles, the Walnut Trail comes in from the left. Stay on the road as it steadily climbs 700 feet from the stream until it reaches the top at an intersection with the Ridge Trail at 5.4 miles. McCarty Road turns left; to the right is a sign for the Ridge Trail, marked with infrequent red blazes.

Turn right on the Ridge Trail, which is fairly open. Ferns grow waist high by August. The trail leads up, then gradually downhill, and is easily followed, though often obstructed by blowdowns. Just after reentering the woods, at 5.6 miles, watch carefully for an old woods road on the left, at a gully. The red blazes are faint, but turn left to follow them, continuing downhill.

Cross another relatively open area with many ferns, then reenter the woods. At 6.8 miles, reach an intersection with a woods road. Turn left, still on the Ridge Trail. Walk around a metal gate and a small cabin on a gravel road. Cross Brunnerdale Run on steppingstones. Turn right on Brunnerdale Road at a black-and-yellow metal gate to reach your car.

42. CHERRY RIDGE TRAIL

Distance	5.7 miles
Elevation	175 feet
Time to hike	2½ hours
Surface	Timber haul roads, old logging road, and railroad grade
Interesting features	Old Loggers Path
Facilities	None
Hunting	Yes

Directions

From US 6 at Towanda:

1. South on connector road (SR 2027, Main Street) for 1.9 miles to US 220
2. Turn left (south) on US 220 for 1.5 miles to PA 414
3. Turn right (west) on PA 414 for 21.6 miles to PA 154
4. Turn left (south) on PA 154 for 11.4 miles to Shunk
5. Turn right on SR 4002 for 3.6 miles to Ellenton (SR 4002 turns into SR 1015 as it crosses into Lycoming County)
6. At a T intersection, turn left on to SR 1013 (a gravel road) for 1.1 miles
7. At a Y intersection, bear right onto Ellenton Ridge Road for .6 mile
8. The parking area is on the left, near a sign reading "Krimm Road–Old Loggers Path"

Coordinates 41°31'37"N; 76°49'53"W

The Old Loggers Path follows the old timbering roads of the Central Pennsylvania Lumber Company and the abandoned narrow-gauge Susquehanna and Eagles Mere Railroad. It is a rugged 27.1-mile circuit trail; the Cherry Ridge Trail is an easier side trail with little elevation change.

When we hiked here in July 1996, the trees had literally been stripped bare by the elm spanworm (family Geometridae, or measuring worms). Elm spanworm larvae hatch from eggs and develop a little more rapidly than those of the gypsy moth. The familiar inchworms defoliate the trees in spring and early summer. The adult, a white moth, begins to appear in late June. Peak flight and

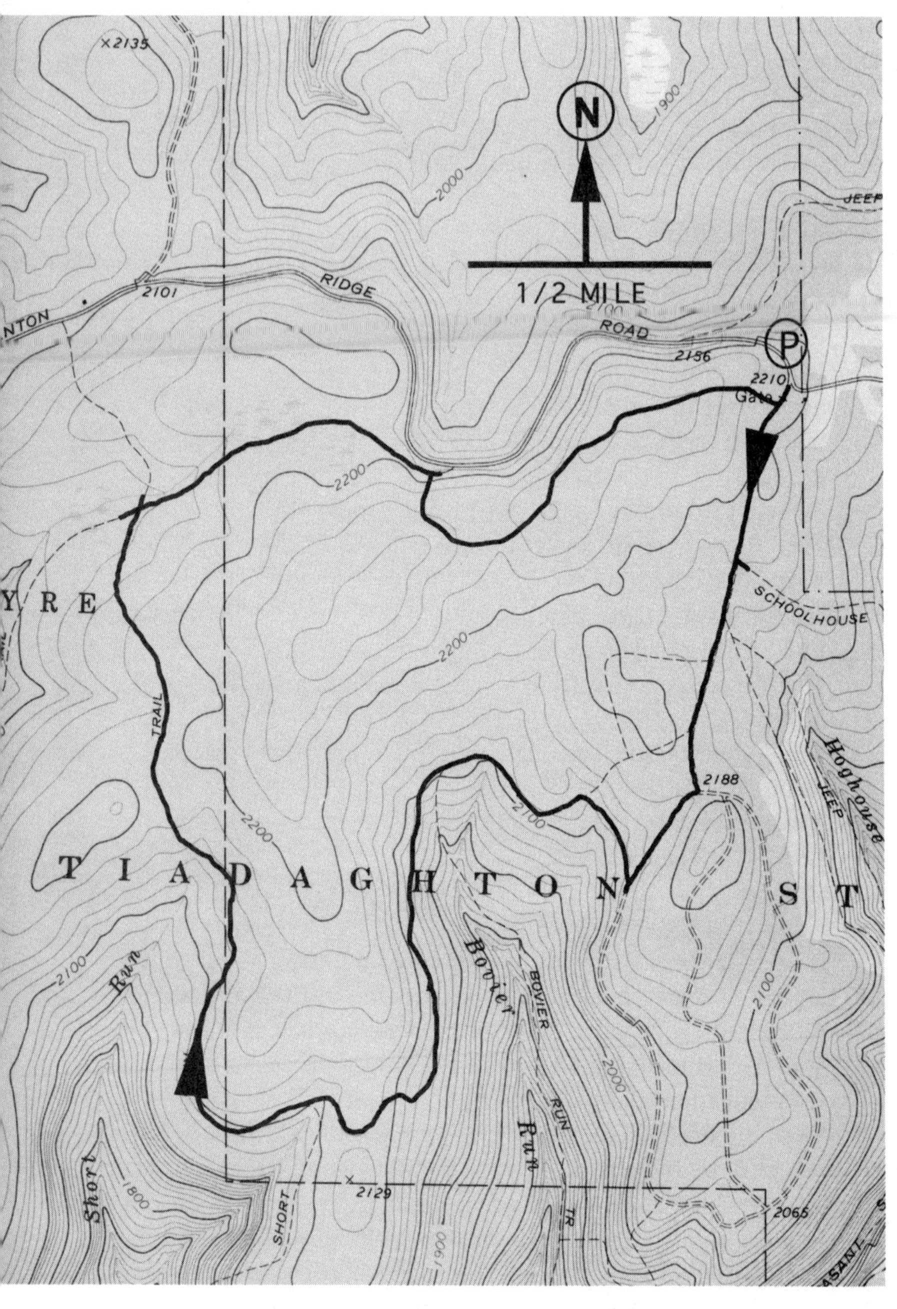
×2135
2101
NTON
RIDGE
1/2 MILE
2100
ROAD
2156
2210
Gate
2000
1900
JEEP
2200
YRE
SCHOOLHOUSE
TRAIL
2200
2188
Hoghouse
JEEP
2100
2200
TIADAGHTON ST
Run
2100
Bovier
BOVIER
RUN
2000
2100
Run
Short
1800
SHORT
2129
1900
TR
2065

mating occur in early July. They are attracted to lights, and their swarm has been compared to a snowstorm.

The natural biological enemies of the elm spanworm are two egg parasites. Ground beetles and wasp and fly parasites also attack the larvae and pupae stages. As infestation reaches epidemic size, these predators are usually able to bring an outbreak under control within a year or so. However, the most recent outbreak began in 1991, and Lycoming County was at the center of the area of defoliation. Five years of infestation caused many trees to die. At last, it appears that the epidemic is over. In 1999, we saw no evidence of the inchworm or adult moth, and a forest canopy is reemerging.

Begin the hike by walking around the yellow-and-black metal gate on the woods road at a sign for the Cherry Ridge Trail. Your return route is just to the right. The Old Loggers Path is orange-blazed. The Cherry Ridge side trail is blue-blazed.

At .2 mile, another woods trail comes in from the left at a functional trail register—a metal ammo box. This trail leads 1.7 miles to the ghost town of Masten, the starting point of the Old Loggers Path. From 1900 to 1930, Masten was a prosperous sawmill logging town, then a Civilian Conservation Corps camp. You lose the orange blazes here; the trail becomes entirely blue-blazed.

The woods road turns right at a wildlife study area behind an electrified fence. The fence keeps out deer and humans. The area behind the fence contains thick shrubs and small to medium hardwoods, though no mature trees. The spanworm preferentially attacks oaks and maples. On your right there are a few beeches, black cherries, and hickories, many dead trees, and little understory growth.

There is evidence of road building and logging activity as the road turns right away from the fence. Watch carefully for the double blue blazes indicating turns. Cherry Ridge on your right has been stripped bare of trees by the elm spanworm. More of the trees at lower elevations to your left escaped devastation. The Forest Service is clearing out the dead and dying trees. The road continues just below the ridgeline. Watch carefully for a blue arrow on a tree for a right turn up another timber haul road.

As the road turns right again at 2 miles, the blue blazes enter the woods. Defoliation has allowed considerable light to filter through, and ferns sometimes obscure the path. Although hardly recognizable as such, this is a long-abandoned logging road.

The trail leads west, then north. Smaller beech trees are damaged, and there are stands of hemlocks, but no oaks whatsoever. The lack of a forest canopy has encouraged the growth of ground pine, club moss, sphagnum, and other mosses in moist areas, and ferns in drier areas. Cross two small streams.

At 4.2 miles, turn right at an intersection of woods roads, following a blue arrow on a tree. For a short distance, you are walking in a rocky seasonal stream, a tributary of Long Run. Soon the trail levels to an old railroad grade, cut into the hillside. Well constructed with rocks, the grade is evident. There is a great deal of striped maple (moosewood) along the trail—not a true maple at all, but a shrub or small tree that appears resistant to the spanworm. At 4.9 miles, you leave the grade at a blue arrow to turn right into the woods.

At 5.7 miles, you complete the loop at the metal gate and your car.

PART FIVE

NATURE TRAILS

These trails are all 2 miles or less in length. For most, you can pick up a trail guide at the trailhead or at the park office. They offer all sorts of features: lakes, waterfalls, swamps, virgin forests, wetlands, fine views. These short hikes are fun and educational for kids—and enjoyable for anyone who'd like to get the flavor of the outdoors in a unique area in an hour or less.

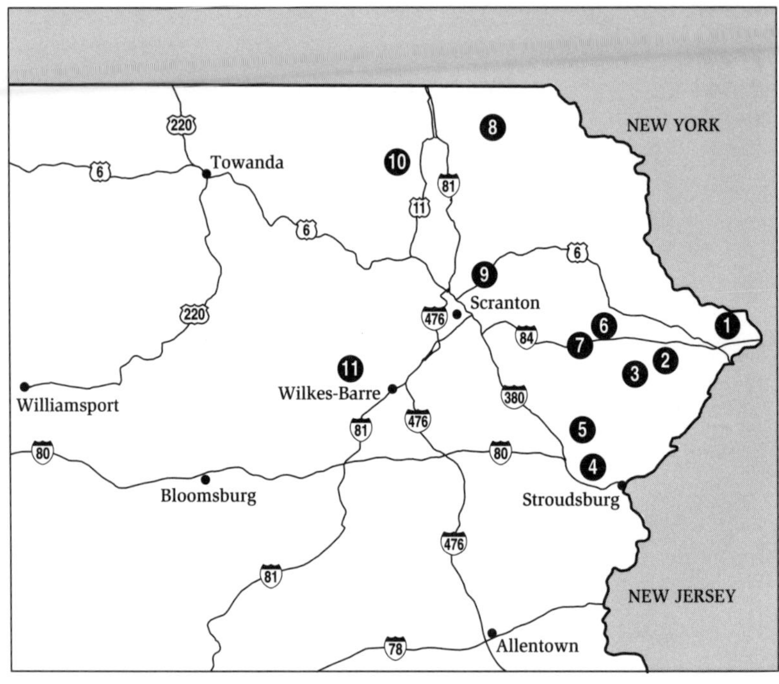

1. Moon Lake
2. Buckhorn Fire Tower–State Game Lands 209
3. Tarkill Interpretive Trail
4. Rattlesnake Creek Falls
5. North Woods and Fern Ridge Trails at Tannersville
6. Lacawac Sanctuary
7. Ledgedale Natural Area
8. Woodbourne Forest and Wildlife Sanctuary
9. Florence Shelly Preserve
10. Conservation Island–Promised Land State Park
11. Archbald Pothole State Park

1. BUCKHORN FIRE TOWER–STATE GAME LANDS 209

Distance	2 miles
Elevation	310 feet
Time to hike	1 hour
Surface	Grassy woods road
Interesting features	Fire tower, views
Facilities	None
Hunting	Yes

Directions

From I-84 (Exit 10) near the New Jersey line:

1. East on US 6 for .8 mile to Schocopee Road, at a sign for the Black Walnut Country Inn
2. Turn left on Schocopee Road for .7 mile to Fire Tower Road (TR 430)
3. Bear right on Fire Tower Road for 1.7 miles; the asphalt road changes to a rocky, rough dirt road
4. Park at 3.9 miles (total), at the sign "Buckhorn Fire Tower"

Coordinates 41°23'43"N; 74°49'26"W

You reach the trailhead for this hike, located in State Game Lands 209, after a mile of rough driving on a rocky dirt road. Walk west around the yellow metal gate, following a woods road closed to traffic. Mixed second-growth hardwoods and white birches alternate along the trail. On our visit in May, we had to look down frequently to avoid stepping on numerous red efts. The very rocky road leads uphill through patches of pine and spruce trees to the top of Buckhorn Ridge.

Pass a nonoperating well and pump. The Buckhorn Fire Tower, just ahead, is about 70 feet high, and there are fine views of the mountains from the top.

Turn south past the fire tower to a trail. Continue downhill through huckleberries and pines to a swamp and Pinchot Brook at 1 mile. The trail peters out here and becomes almost impossible to follow. Turn around and backtrack to the fire tower and your car.

2. TARKILL INTERPRETIVE TRAIL

Distance	.6 mile
Elevation	30 feet
Time to hike	20 minutes
Surface	Woods trail
Interesting features	Interpretive nature trail
Facilities	Outhouse
Hunting	Yes

Directions

From I-84 (Exit 8) between Scranton and the New Jersey–New York line:

1. South on PA 402 for 4.3 miles
2. Turn right into parking area just before guardrail

Coordinates 41°18'34"N; 75°06'31"W

This is a new and interesting nature trail built in May 1998. Located on just thirty acres in Delaware State Forest, the trail winds through a stand of young hardwoods, mature hemlocks, and a white pine plantation. At the parking lot, pick up a guide keyed to twenty-seven numbered stops along the trail. At post 2, make sure you turn *right* and follow the blue blazed trail. Some trees are marked white; these are saved when the Bureau of Forestry conducts a selective harvest. The terrain is gentle through wetlands along Tarkill Creek and drier upland woods.

3. CONSERVATION ISLAND–PROMISED LAND STATE PARK

Distance	1 mile
Elevation	Minimal
Time to hike	30 minutes
Surface	Level woods road, rocky trail
Interesting features	Promised Land Lake, hemlock and rhododendron forest
Facilities	None
Hunting	No

Directions

From PA 390 at Visitors Center:

1. Pickerel Point Road east for .5 mile
2. Turn left on Park Avenue for .6 mile to parking lot on the right

Coordinates 41°17'58"N; 75°12'02"W

This level trail takes you through a hemlock and rhododendron forest typical of the Poconos, and around an island in the middle of Promised Land Lake. Stop at the Promised Land Visitors Center and ask for both a park recreation guide and a guide to the Nature Trail.

From the Conservation Island parking lot, cross a culvert to the island. Signs direct you on the Nature Trail, with numbered posts corresponding to points of interest in the guide booklet. The trail is rocky in places. Those with strollers or using wheelchairs may prefer to stay on the level woods road that circles the island.

4. NORTH WOODS AND FERN RIDGE TRAILS AT TANNERSVILLE

Distance 2 miles
Elevation 130 feet
Time to hike 1 hour
Surface Woodland trails
Interesting features Nature trail
Facilities Benches along North Woods Trail; no water or rest rooms
Hunting No

Directions

From I-80 (Exit 45) near Stroudsburg:

1. North on PA 715 for .5 mile to PA 611
2. Turn right (south) on PA 611 for .9 mile to Cherry Lane Road
3. Turn left on Cherry Lane Road (SR 1001) for 2.6 miles to Bog Road
4. Turn right on Bog Road (509A) for .5 mile to the pull-off on the left side of the road

Coordinates 41°02'41"N; 75°15'30"W

The self-guiding North Woods Trail is marked with wooden arrow signs. Walk uphill 200 feet to a large trail sign and pick up the trail guide available there. Numbered posts correspond to the guide.

The upland forest is composed of beeches; white, red, and chestnut oaks; and red maples in moist areas. The trail later passes through a dark hemlock forest, edged with white pines and birches. Return to the road at .8 mile.

Turn left past your car and walk .2 mile on the road, crossing Cranberry Creek. On the right side at a small pull-off, Fern Ridge Trail leads into the woods. The trail is not blazed, but windfalls are placed along the trail to block trails no longer in use. The last .2 mile follows the south side of Cranberry Creek and contains much of the vegetation also found in the bog, including sphagnum moss, black spruce, pitcher plants, and tamaracks.

For more information, contact the Nature Conservancy, 1211 Chestnut Street, 12th Floor, Philadelphia, PA 19107, 215-963-1400. Or you can write to the Monroe County Conservation District, 8050 Running Valley Road, Stroudsburg, PA 18360, 717-629-3061.

5. RATTLESNAKE CREEK FALLS

Distance	2 miles
Elevation	350 feet
Time to hike	1 hour
Surface	Rocky woods road
Interesting features	Rattlesnake Creek Falls, blueberries in July and August, thick stands of mountain and sheep laurel and rhododendron
Facilities	None
Hunting	Yes

Directions

From I-380 (Exit 8) near Scranton:

1. East on PA 940 for 5.4 miles to PA 390
2. Turn left (north) on PA 390 for 1.2 miles to PA 191 at stop sign
3. Turn left (north) on PA 191 and PA 390 for 2.1 miles
4. PA 390 goes straight ahead; bear left, staying on PA 191 for another .1 mile
5. Turn left on Monomonack Road for .1 mile to Pleasant Ridge Road
6. Bear right on Pleasant Ridge Road for .9 mile to the end of the road and the parking lot for State Game Lands 221

Coordinates 41°10'48"N; 75°17'17"W

Walk northwest past the metal gate uphill on a rocky road. Rattlesnake Creek is to your right. At .2 mile, cross Rattlesnake Creek on rocks. The road follows the creek for a short distance, then veers away. The trail is lined with blueberries and sheep laurel, which blooms pink in early June. Mixed oaks, birches, beeches, and ferns grow in the sandy, rocky soil. After a steady uphill climb, at .9 mile reach a trail intersection with a woods road. Turn left (south) to the end of the road and a fire ring. Steps lead down to the falls in a 100-foot-deep hemlock- and mountain laurel-filled ravine. A rope assists you in rappelling 75 feet down into the gorge. Rattlesnake Falls is to the right. Climb back up the steep trail. An unmarked trail follows the edge of the ravine for .1 mile, but then peters out. Backtrack to your car.

6. LEDGEDALE NATURAL AREA

Distance	1.5 miles
Elevation	70 feet
Time to hike	45 minutes
Surface	Rocky woods road, old logging roads
Interesting features	Interpretive nature trail
Facilities	Trailside benches
Hunting	Yes

Directions

From I-84 (Exit 6) between Scranton and the New Jersey line:

1. North on PA 507 for .7 mile
2. Turn left on Ledgedale Road (SR 4001) for 1.6 miles to Kuhn Hill Road
3. Turn left on Kuhn Hill Road for .3 mile and turn left into the parking lot

Coordinates 41°22'06"N; 75°19'13"W

There is a total of 2.5 miles of intersecting trails in this 100-acre woodland tract owned by Pennsylvania Power and Light. The trail passes through two major forest types: hemlock and rhododendron forest, and northern hardwood forest consisting mostly of

Downy woodpecker

beech, sugar maple, yellow birch, and white ash. Pick up a trail map at the parking lot. Hikers can construct loops of varying lengths; the longest route along the perimeter of the preserve totals 1.5 miles.

Notice the large number of blowdowns on this hike. Woodpeckers are attracted to the decaying wood. Round holes were made by downy or hairy woodpeckers, large, rectangular ones probably by pileated woodpeckers. You will step over several small streams. If you walk quietly, you might see raccoon tracks, red and gray foxes, red and gray squirrels, and especially, deer.

7. LACAWAC SANCTUARY

Distance	1 mile
Elevation	140 feet
Time to hike	1 hour
Surface	Woods trail and old woods road
Interesting features	Interpretive nature trail
Facilities	None
Hunting	No

Directions

From I-84 (Exit 6) between Scranton and the New Jersey–New York line:

1. North on PA 507 for .7 mile to Ledgedale Road
2. Turn left on Ledgedale Road (SR 4001) for 1.7 miles to a T intersection at a stop sign
3. Turn right (north) on SR 3006 (still Ledgedale Road) for .9 mile to St. Mary Church Road
4. Turn right onto St. Mary Church Road (SR 3013) for .2 mile to Lacawac Road
5. Turn right on Lacawac Road for .6 mile to sign and dirt road to Lacawac Sanctuary
6. Turn right on dirt road .4 mile to the parking area, office, and trailhead to Maurice Broun Nature Trail

Coordinates 41°22'37"N; 75°17'59"W

Lacawac Sanctuary is a 400-acre nature preserve and educational center adjacent to Lake Wallenpaupack. Pick up a well-prepared descriptive brochure at the box at the trailhead at a wildflower meadow reverting to woods. Eleven numbered signs along the trail are keyed to the guide. The trail winds for a 1-mile loop through hemlock and mixed hardwood forest, pastures, and abandoned farmland along Lake Wallenpaupack.

At .2 mile, you reach a ridge overlooking the lake—views are obscured by vegetation in the summer. The Wallenpaupack River valley was used by Indians and later by settlers for transportation and agriculture. This area was also a center in the late nineteenth century for lumber production and leather tanning.

At .8 mile, you may notice an oasis of green on your right, inside a wire fence. Ecologists at the University of Scranton are studying the effect of the many deer here on the vegetation. In 1994–95, "exclosures" were built, each 1.25 acres in size and surrounded by an 8-foot-high fence. The interior of each exclosure is divided into 20-by-20-meter plots, matched to plots outside the fence. The study will continue for ten years, but the impact of the deer is already apparent. The deer have browsed almost everything less than 8 feet from the ground outside the exclosure.

The preserve is also home to turkeys, bears, red and gray foxes, porcupines, snowshoe hares, flying squirrels, and even bobcats. During spring migrations and nesting season, there are many songbirds, especially at the edges of the forest.

Lacawac Lake, within the preserve, is said to be "the southernmost unpolluted glacial lake with remnant acidic bog habitat." Guided tours of the lake are offered at 10:00 A.M. on Saturdays from May through October. For further information, contact Lacawac Sanctuary, RR 1 Box 518, Lake Ariel, PA 18436, or telephone 717-689-9494.

8. FLORENCE SHELLY PRESERVE

Distance	2 miles
Elevation	180 feet
Time to hike	50 minutes
Surface	Old woods road, trail through wetlands and meadow
Interesting features	Wetlands nature preserve
Facilities	None
Hunting	No

Directions

From I-81 (Exit 68) near the New York line: south on PA 171 for 16.1 miles to parking lot on the left

Coordinates 41°52'44"N; 75°31'04"W

This trail offers an interesting look at various types of wetlands—swamp, stream, and wet meadow. Look for a trail sign at the edge of the parking lot. Follow the trail downhill to a muddy jeep trail. Pass a trail intersection (your return route) at a sign for the Thompson Wetlands Nature Conservancy.

Continue on the jeep road straight ahead through hemlocks to aptly named Black Spruce Run. An old stone row fence is on your left. Turn right just before the stream, following the Nature Trail sign through a spruce and scotch pine plantation, followed by a wet meadow.

Plew's Swamp, containing cattail, swamp oak, skunk cabbage, alyssum, willow, rush, sedge, and royal fern, lies just ahead. Complete the Nature Trail Loop at the Thompson Wetlands sign and return to your car.

Ireland Road is .2 mile north of the parking lot. The trail from the Ireland Road parking lot leads to a two-story observation deck overlooking Plew's Swamp.

9. ARCHBALD POTHOLE STATE PARK

Distance	1 mile
Elevation	70 feet
Time to hike	30 minutes
Surface	Shale- and coal-covered mining road
Interesting features	Largest known pothole in the world
Facilities	None
Disability access	No; there are ten steps up to platform for a view of the pothole
Hunting	No

Directions

From I-81 (Exit 57A) in Scranton:

1. East on US 6 for 6 miles (past Eynon Plaza and the Jeep dealer on the right)
2. Archbald Pothole State Park is on the right

Coordinates 41°30'44"N; 75°34'23"W

This huge hole in the earth was formed 15,000 years ago in the same way as potholes in your street—by melting ice. Glacial water swirled down a 200-foot crack in the bedrock, like water down a bathtub drain. This resulted in a 38-foot-deep pothole cut through sandstone, shale, and coal.

Archbald Pothole was discovered in 1884 by coal miners while extending a mine shaft and was briefly used as a ventilation shaft for the mine. The elliptical pothole is at the end of the parking lot, and you get a good view of it from a large platform. The water first wore away the top layer of bedrock, which is sandstone. Next, the swirling water and rock carved through gray shale, leaving a particularly smooth and polished surface. The bottom layer is black anthracite coal. Exposed to the weather since 1884, the pothole is gradually eroding. Ferns, mosses, and lichens have colonized the rock ledges. There is snow and ice at the bottom even in late spring.

Begin your hike near the entrance to the park, turning right on an old mining road. There are no marked boundaries for the park, which is only 150 acres. Follow the road around the edge of the park past many large sinkholes, slag piles, and tailings. Strip-mining of the anthracite coalfield is evidenced by culm—piles of broken rock that was removed to get at the coal. You will find piles of culm 50 feet high or more, all around Luzerne and Lackawanna Counties. Although it contains almost no plant nutrients, the culm is eventually colonized, mostly by birch, aspen, and weeds.

The vegetation is stunted because of the very poor soil conditions and consists mainly of clumps of paper birch and scrub oak. The interior lands of the park are undergoing strip-mine reclamation. These areas will be used for outdoor recreation and will include athletic fields. Several trails to the left lead you back to the parking lot at the edge of the area of reclamation.

10. WOODBOURNE FOREST AND WILDLIFE SANCTUARY

Distance	1 mile
Elevation	75 feet
Time to hike	45 minutes
Surface	Woodland trail
Interesting features	Climax forest, 16-acre alder swamp, many eastern hemlocks 200 to 400 years old
Facilities	Benches along trails; no water or rest rooms; no picnicking, smoking, camping, or pets permitted
Hunting	No

Directions

From I-81 (Exit 67) north of Scranton:

1. West on PA 492 toward New Milford for .65 mile to stop sign (end of PA 492)
2. Turn left (south) on US 11 for 1 mile to PA 706
3. Bear right (west) on PA 706 for 7.1 miles to PA 29
4. Turn left (south) on PA 29 for 6.4 miles to Woodbourne on the left

Coordinates 41°45'41"N; 75°53'53"W

Within Woodbourne Forest and Wildlife Sanctuary, only 600 acres in size, is the largest remaining stand of virgin forest known in northeastern Pennsylvania. A trail guide is available from the register box at the edge of the parking lot. The booklet explains the ecology of the area and will help you identify some of the 303 plant varieties found in the preserve. Forty small red-numbered posts along the trail are matched to the trail guide.

The Nature Trail leads north from the parking area, diagonally down across an open field. The numbered posts begin at a stone row at the edge of another field. At .2 mile, you reach the edge of the 16-acre alder swamp. Bleak skeletal trees arising from the misty swamp create an otherworldly effect and remind one of an old movie set, perhaps *Creatures from the Black Lagoon.* The swamp began at the end of the last ice age as a melting block of ice left behind when the glacier withdrew north 12,000 years ago. But it is a beaver family that maintains the water level, creating the perfect environment for many wetland plants and animals.

A catwalk crosses a portion of swamp, and the trail then winds through a section of virgin forest. The dominant tree species is eastern hemlock; many are 200 to 400 years old and more than 100 feet high. You also find American beech and red maple, with smaller numbers of yellow birch, sugar maple, white ash, black cherry, and red oak.

For further information, contact the Nature Conservancy, RR 6 Box 6294, Montrose, PA 18801, or telephone 717-278-3384

11. MOON LAKE

Distance 1 mile
Elevation 75 feet
Time to hike 1 hour
Surface Rocky woods trail
Interesting features Family recreational facilities
Facilities Picnic tables, grills; water, rest rooms at marina
Hunting No

Directions

From US 11 in Wilkes-Barre:

1. North on PA 309 for 5.8 miles to PA 415
2. PA 309 veers right; continue straight ahead north on PA 415 for 2.2 miles to PA 118
3. Turn left (west) on PA 118 for 6.5 miles to PA 29
4. Turn left (south) on PA 29 for 4.4 miles to Lake Silkworth Road
5. Turn right on Lake Silkworth Road (SR 4001) for .2 mile; continue straight ahead on park entrance road for .7 mile to park entrance

Coordinates 41°15'17"N; 76°03'22"W

Moon Lake County Park comprises 600 acres of fields and forest that surround a 48-acre lake. Children can learn much about natural history on the Nature's Way Trail. Numbered posts on the trail identify thirty points of interest, including geologic features, plants, and animals. Trail guide booklets are available at the park office. The easy, 1-mile hiking trail begins opposite the park office.

Besides the hiking trail, Moon Lake offers tennis and basketball courts, a swimming pool, camping, ball fields, a stocked lake for fishing, and environmental programs. In the winter, families can enjoy ice skating, sledding, ice fishing, and cross-country skiing. For further information, contact Moon Lake County Park, RD 2 Box 301, Hunlock Creek, PA 18621, or telephone 717-477-5467 or 717-256-3212.

APPENDIXES

DISABILITY ACCESS

These fifteen trails are at least partially accessible to wheelchair hikers. Additionally, service roads in state parks normally closed to the public may be used by those with disabilities to gain access to the park. Contact the state park for permission of the park manager.

1. DINGMANS AND SILVERTHREAD FALLS (Hike No. 1)

The Dingmans Falls area was heavily damaged by storms in 1997–98 and reopened July 2, 1998. The rebuilt wooden boardwalk and viewing platforms are completely accessible and better than ever. The boardwalk trail leads from the rebuilt Visitors Center for a .5-mile round-trip past the two waterfalls.

Directions to the trailhead from I-84 near the New Jersey line: (1) PA 739 south for 13.9 miles, (2) turn right (south) on PA 209 for .1 mile, (3) turn right on Johnny Bee Road for .4 mile, (4) turn right on Dingmans Falls Road for .6 mile (41°13'45"N; 74°53'14"W).

2. BIG POCONO (Hike No. 12)

Accessible for 1.5 mile from Camelback Road on South Trail to intersection with North Trail (rough but possible).

3. TOBYHANNA STATE PARK (Hike No. 15)

The entire 5.1-mile trail around lake is accessible.

4. GOULDSBORO STATE PARK (Hike No. 16)

Follow State Park Road 1.3 miles from the park entrance on PA 507 (on the boat access road) to a gravel pull-off beside a yellow gate with a sign reading "Old Entrance Road." Go around the gate to an abandoned asphalt road. The road continues for .8 mile of easy rolling to a T intersection with abandoned Route 611. Here you can turn either right or left for another 1.5 miles to the park boundary (some broken and overgrown pavement).

5. BRADY'S LAKE (Hike No. 17)

Accessible for the first .6 mile, on an asphalt path across the dam, and on the woods road along the lake.

6. SWITCHBACK RAILROAD (Hike No. 23)

Accessible on the railroad grade, except for the climb up Mount Pisgah and the Hacklebernie Mine collapse at 6.8 miles.

7. HAWK MOUNTAIN (Hike No. 25)

The first 300 yards (.2 mile) from the parking lot leads to a special wheelchair-accessible lookout.

8. LOCUST LAKE (Hike No. 26)

The 3-mile paved path around the lake is accessible.

9. LAKE SCRANTON (Hike No. 27)

The entire hike is accessible, including the 3.5-mile asphalt path around lake and the .1-mile gravel path from the parking lot. The lake may be fished *only* by those requiring assistance in casting a line. The handicapped-accessible fishing pier is accessed from a separate parking lot. Call Allied Services at 717-348-1332 for permission.

10. SEVEN TUBS (Hike No. 29)

The first two "tubs" on Wheelbarrow Run can be easily reached on a paved trail and then a wooden footbridge for the first .1 mile. However, from here the hike is not accessible to wheelchair hikers.

11. RIVERSIDE COMMONS (Hike No. 32)

Accessible, except for difficult crossings of Market and Pierce Streets.

12. EAGLES MERE (Hike No. 37)

The first 1.2 mile is a level railroad grade. Although deeply rutted, it is passable. The rest of the trail is not accessible.

13. CHILISUAGI TRAIL (Hike No. 39)

The entire trail, including the side trail to the fossil pit and the Ridgefield Point Loop, is accessible. The trail surface is gravel, crushed stone, wood chips, and mown grass. There are some hilly sections.

14. CONSERVATION ISLAND–PROMISED LAND STATE PARK (Nature Trail No. 3)

The entire 1-mile trail is accessible on a level woods road around the island. The Nature Trail is not accessible.

15. ARCHBALD POTHOLE (Nature Trail No. 9)

There is a ramp to view the pothole, which is adjacent to the parking lot.

HIKE MAP INDEX

The U.S. Geological Survey maps (7.5-minute quadrangles) from which the maps of the forty-two hikes are derived are listed here, by hike number and name.

Hike No.	*Hike Name*	*Map Sheet(s)*
1	Dingmans Falls	Lake Maskenozha, PA
2	Pocono Environmental Education Center	Lake Maskenozha, PA
3	Shohola Falls	Shohola, PA Rowlands, PA
4	Delaware Water Gap	Stroudsburg, PA
5	Pennel Run	Twelvemile Pond, PA Skytop, PA
6	Stillwater Natural Area	Twelvemile Pond, PA Lake Maskenozha, PA
7	Blooming Grove 4-H Trail	Hawley, PA
8	Bruce Lake Natural Area	Promised Land, PA
9	Shuman Point Natural Area	Hawley, PA
10	Promised Land State Park	Promised Land, PA
11	Tannersville Cranberry Bog	Mount Pocono, PA
12	Big Pocono State Park	Mount Pocono, PA
13	Devil's Hole	Buck Hill Falls, PA
14	Wolf Swamp and Deep Lake	Mount Pocono, PA Pocono Pines, PA
15	Tobyhanna State Park	Tobyhanna, PA
16	Gouldsboro State Park	Tobyhanna, PA

Hike No.	*Hike Name*	*Map Sheet(s)*
17	Brady's Lake	Thornurst, PA
18	Big Pine Hill	Pleasant View Summit, PA
19	Choke Creek Trail	Pleasant View Summit, PA
20	Margy's Trail	Blakeslee, PA
21	Beltzville State Park	Palmerton, PA
22	Hickory Run State Park	Hickory Run, PA
23	Switchback Railroad	Lehighton, PA Nesquehoning, PA
24	Glen Onoko Run	Weatherly, PA
25	Hawk Mountain Sanctuary	New Ringgold, PA
26	Locust Lake State Park	Shenandoah, PA Delano, PA
27	Lake Scranton	Scranton, PA Olyphant, PA
28	Lackawanna State Park	Dalton, PA
29	Seven Tubs Nature Area	Wilkes-Barre East, PA
30	Frances Slocum State Park	Kingston, PA
31	Nescopeck Ponds Loop	Freeland, PA White Haven, PA
32	Riverside Commons	Kingston, PA Wilkes-Barre West, PA
33	Ricketts Glen State Park	Red Rock, PA
34	Great Bend	Great Bend, PA
35	Salt Springs State Park	Franklin Forks, PA-NY
36	Joe Gmiter Trail	Noxen, PA
37	Eagles Mere	Eagles Mere, PA
38	Worlds End State Park	Eagles Mere, PA
39	Chilisuagi Trail	Washingtonville, PA
40	Mount Pisgah	East Troy, PA
41	Loyalsock Trail	Hillsgrove, PA
42	Cherry Ridge Trail	Grover, PA

Nature Trails

Hike No.	*Hike Name*	*Map Sheet(s)*
1	Buckhorn Fire Tower–State Game Lands 209	Pond Eddy, PA
2	Tarkill Interpretive Trail	Pecks Pond, PA
3	Conservation Island–Promised Land State Park	Promised Land, PA
4	North Woods and Fern Ridge Trails at Tannersville	Mount Pocono, PA
5	Rattlesnake Creek Falls	Buck Hill Falls, PA
6	Ledgedale Natural Area	Newfoundland, PA
7	Lacawac Sanctuary	Lakeview, PA
8	Florence Shelley Preserve	Susquehanna, PA-NY
9	Archbald Pothole State Park	Carbondale, PA
10	Woodbourne Forest and Wildlife Sanctuary	Montrose West, PA
11	Moon Lake	Nanticoke, PA Harveys Lake, PA

SOURCES OF MAPS AND INFORMATION

Pennsylvania Department of Transportation
Distribution Services Unit
6th Floor—Forum Place
555 Walnut Street
Harrisburg, PA 17101
Free state maps are available that show cities, towns, roads, state forests, parks, game lands, and major trails.

Pennsylvania Game Commission
Department MS
2001 Elmerton Avenue
Harrisburg, PA 17110-9797
www.pgc.state.pa.us
Individual state game lands maps are $1 each.

Department of Conservation and Natural Resources
Bureau of State Parks
P.O. Box 8551
Harrisburg, PA 17106-8551
www.dcnr.state.pa.us
Recreational guides, including maps, for each state park in the system are available free of charge.

Department of Conservation and Natural Resources
Bureau of Forestry
P.O. Box 8552
Harrisburg, PA 17106-8552
www.dcnr.state.pa.us
Maps for state forests, including the Wyoming, Delaware, Lackawanna, and Tiadaghton State Forests in northeastern Pennsylvania, are available free of charge.

United States Geological Survey 7.5-minute topographical quadrangle maps cover the entire state. They are available in larger map stores. You can also call 1-800-USA-MAPS for ordering information.